Monitoring, Assessment, Recording, Reporting and Accountability

Meeting the Standards

SECOND EDITION

Rita Headington

David Fulton Publishers

David Fulton Publishers Ltd
The Chiswick Centre, 414 Chiswick High Road, London W4 5TF

www.fultonpublishers.co.uk

First published in Great Britain in 2000 by David Fulton Publishers
Second edition 2003

The right of Rita Headington to be identified as the author of this work has been
asserted by her in accordance with the Copyright, Designs and Patents Act 1988.

David Fulton Publishers is a division of Granada Learning Limited, part of
Granada plc.

British Library Cataloguing in Publication Data
A catalogue record for this book is available from the British Library.

ISBN 1-85346-962-9

Typeset by FiSH Books, London
Printed and bound in Great Britain

Contents

Foreword

When Rita Headington invited me to write the foreword to this thoughtful book, she explained that the impetus for it stemmed from her own experience of trying, without success, to find a single text that addressed current issues in assessment in a style that suited newly qualified teachers and trainee teachers. She has very successfully produced such a text. I am very pleased to write the foreword to a book that manages to deal with a complex field in such a direct, clear, comprehensive and accessible way.

Few, if any, aspects of education have received more attention than assessment in the past decade. We know, for example, that assessment is important for learning. In particular, we know that a specific kind of assessment – formative assessment – improves learning. We also know, however, that this kind of assessment is not always done well in practice and that policy makers have underestimated the difficulty of implementing it effectively. The way we assess learning has changed such that we are now more aware of the need to ensure pupils get a chance to demonstrate what they know, understand and can do. Teachers and pupils themselves are expected to play a more active role in the assessment process and assessments are expected to reflect how learning happens. As a result there is a far greater range of assessment types and modes in use and we are better at distinguishing different purposes of assessment. The language of assessment reflects this diversity – we talk, for instance, about formative and summative assessment, assessment for accountability and assessment for diagnosing learning strengths and weaknesses.

This book explains, exemplifies and discusses all these facets of assessment in a reasoned and down-to-earth style. It does not underestimate the demands placed on teachers and trainee teachers to make assessment work. It provides the necessary foundation on which to build and sustain sound assessment practice. It tackles a host of interrelated assessment issues – monitoring, recording, reporting and accountability – but it doesn't lose sight of the overall aim of assessment which is to enhance learning. The theme of learning is there on every page with definitions, descriptions and examples of, for example, learning objectives, learning outcomes, different types of learning, and accounts of how formative assessments feed back to learning and teaching.

The naive student teacher could be forgiven for thinking that assessment is an end in itself, given the emphasis placed upon it in the media and the assumption often made by politicians that assessment on its own will yield 'higher standards'. A significant characteristic of assessment in this book is that assessment information is only as good as the use to which it is put. The activities and mini case studies, in particular, model this principle: they engage the reader in reflecting upon and making judgements about their own and others' learning and assessment contexts. In addition, assessment guidance links with the policy context in which the teacher works and into which the newly qualified teacher is inducted. In this regard, the Literacy and Numeracy Strategies, National Curriculum assessment – both standard assessment tasks/tests and teacher assessment – target setting and baseline assessment are explained and discussed.

Only very recently have policy makers begun to realise that the kind of assessment that now needs to be prioritised in this country is assessment *for* learning. For example, the new Ofsted guidance for inspecting schools, that was published in 2000, acknowledges this quite explicitly. The upshot for teachers is their increased role in the assessment enterprise with a consequent need for them to appreciate the power they have to influence learning in their classrooms. This book assumes little knowledge of current issues in assessment on the part of the reader, but it takes the reader through the complexities of the various elements of assessment to a sophisticated understanding that is a prerequisite to implementing quality assessment in practice.

Professor Kathy Hall
Leeds Metropolitan University
March 2000

Acknowledgements

I would like to thank the many pupils, trainees, teachers and colleagues who have assisted me in developing the ideas and materials within *Monitoring, Assessment, Recording, Reporting and Accountability: Meeting the Standards*.

My particular thanks go to:

- the pupils whose work has been used to demonstrate different aspects of MARRA;
- the trainee teachers and NQTs who allowed me to use their records, especially Anne, Joyce and Sharon;
- colleagues who, across the years, have contributed to my knowledge and understanding of assessment, particularly those in the Buckinghamshire Advisory Service and at Canterbury Christ Church University College;
- Alexis Yates, for producing several figures and extending my knowledge of ICT;
- Trisha David, Carol Aubrey, Maggie Last and Allison Cackett for reading the text as it developed and providing critical feedback;
- Kathy Hall for giving of her time so generously to write the Foreword.

Abbreviations

DfES	Department for Education and Skills
EAL	English as an Additional Language
HMI	Her Majesty's Inspectorate
IEP	Individual Education Plan
INSET	In-Service Training
LD	Level Descriptions
LEA	Local Education Authority
LSA	Learning Support Assistant
MARRA	Monitoring, Assessment, Recording, Reporting and Accountability
NLS	National Literacy Strategy
NNS	National Numeracy Strategy
NQT	Newly Qualified Teacher
OFSTED	Office for Standards in Education
OMR	Optical Mark Reader
QCA	Qualifications and Curriculum Authority
QTS	Qualified Teacher Status
RoA	Record of Achievement
SCAA	School Curriculum and Assessment Authority (subsumed by QCA)
SEAC	School Examination and Assessment Council (subsumed by SCAA)
SEN	Special Educational Needs
SENCO	Special Educational Needs Coordinator
SoA	Statement of Attainment
TGAT	Task Group for Assessment and Testing
TTA	Teacher Training Agency
UPN	Unique Pupil Number

CHAPTER 1

An introduction to MARRA

> The most important single factor influencing learning is what the learner already knows. Ascertain this and teach him accordingly.
>
> (Ausubel 1968)

1.1 What is MARRA?

To be awarded Qualified Teacher Status (QTS), those training to teach must meet nationally defined Professional Standards (DfES/TTA 2002). To successfully complete the induction period Newly Qualified Teachers (NQTs) must meet nationally defined Induction Standards (DfES/TTA 2003). The title of this book, *Monitoring, Assessment, Recording, Reporting and Accountability* – MARRA – originates from the initial version of the national standards (DfEE 1998a; TTA 2000).

MARRA is evident across the QTS and Induction Standards, from setting 'high expectations of all pupils' and communicating 'sensitively with parents and carers', to 'understanding how pupils' learning can be affected by their linguistic development', planning from evidence of 'past and current achievement' and promoting 'active and independent learning'. It is considered in greater detail in the section named 'Monitoring and Assessment'.

All aspects of MARRA relate to assessment, which in turn relates to learning. Monitoring is the skill of effectively overviewing and analysing a learning situation. Assessment is the closer examination of pupils' learning. Recording enables teachers to keep track of areas identified by monitoring and assessment including pupils' strengths and weaknesses and their attainment of learning targets. Reporting is the process of informing others about the learning which has taken place. Accountability enables others to evaluate the work of the organisation by analysing the results of assessment.

MARRA underpins professional practice. The national standards that trainee teachers and NQTs must meet provide a starting point for this, focusing on the development of effective practice in assessment and learning coupled with knowledge of, and increasing experience in, the statutory requirements in assessment and reporting. Experienced practitioners build upon these standards to enhance their practice and to make use of statutory assessment results in and beyond the school for the purposes of professional accountability.

1.2 What is the purpose of MARRA?

The purpose of MARRA is to enable learning, teaching and accountability through the effective use of assessment. The Task Group for Assessment and Testing (TGAT), which was convened to consider how the two areas would develop within a national framework, stated that the four purposes of assessment were formative, diagnostic, summative and evaluative (DES 1988).

Formative assessment informs future teaching and learning and is at the heart of practice in the classroom. For example, the teacher may discover, when questioning pupils, that several have misunderstood an explanation. She may decide to intervene and provide teaching which will address the difficulty and so improve pupils' learning. The time taken between assessment and action will vary. Sometimes action is taken almost immediately, with the act of assessment being barely discernible to the untrained observer. At other times the teacher will reflect at length upon pupils' work and design a new or modified teaching programme to enhance learning.

Diagnostic assessment diagnoses the cause of a particular problem and is usually related to individuals rather than groups of pupils. It may take several stages before a diagnosis of a problem is made. For example, when marking the teacher may notice a number of errors occur when a pupil is undertaking word problems in mathematics. While observing she may see that the pupil is not impeded by his reading ability but is far from confident in deciding which method to apply. When she questions the pupil she may discover that he is looking for clues in the individual words rather than considering the problem as a whole, assuming that 'altogether' means 'add' without considering how it is used in the question. The diagnosis can now provide the teacher with sufficient evidence upon which to base teaching which will help the pupil tackle his difficulty. In more extreme cases a teacher may be unable to effectively diagnose a difficulty and call upon the help of the school Special Education Needs Coordinator (SENCO) or an external expert, who in turn may draw upon a range of commercially produced diagnostic assessment material to determine the specific needs of a pupil in a given area of learning. This may in turn lead to a more formalised Individual Education Plan (IEP) which sets specific targets for the pupil's learning.

Summative assessment provides a summation of learning, usually at an end point or on a particular date as in the case of statutory End of Key Stage assessments of the core subjects (see Table 1.1). Summative assessment often marks the point when pupils' results, scores, grades or marks are presented to those beyond the classroom, such as the pupils' parents. If summative assessments occur regularly and relate to one another, parents can experience an overview of their child's learning. If a series of summative assessments do not relate to one another however, parents are left with no more than a meaningless assortment of numbers and letters.

Table 1.1 End of Key Stage Assessments

End of Key Stage	Age	Average level	National tasks and tests	Teacher Assessment
1	7	2	• English • Mathematics	• English • Mathematics • Science
2	11	4	• English • Mathematics • Science	• English • Mathematics • Science

Evaluative assessment focuses upon evaluating the progress of the institution by collating and analysing the progress made by individuals or groups of pupils at and between statutory assessments. In a school situation this process will usually involve the head teacher, senior teachers and the governing body rather than all members of staff, but all teachers should be aware of the issues pertaining to this area, as the results of analysis are used to justify the work of the institution to parents and the wider community. Evaluative assessment enables accountability.

The QTS and Induction standards draw upon the four TGAT purposes by indicating the knowledge, skills and understanding required of new entrants to primary teaching in monitoring, assessment, recording, reporting and accountability. The key to MARRA is not simply knowing and understanding the processes involved and developing the requisite skills in each area, but also having the ability, willingness and flexibility to relate them appropriately to individual pupils, classes, schools and situations. For trainee teachers and NQTs this necessarily begins by working with pupils in the classroom and developing skills in formative and diagnostic assessment. As the examples in Figure 1.1 illustrate, the learning needs of pupils in a class may differ considerably and the teacher needs to use her knowledge of individuals to determine what to teach and how to teach. The planning and assessment cycles detail the processes involved.

Wesley had behavioural difficulties and did not settle to tasks for more than a few minutes particularly if writing was involved. He was given additional support in reading and writing. Wesley enjoyed playing games but lacked social skills when playing with his peers. The teacher decided to develop Wesley's experience and fluency in mental addition by playing a short oral game with him at intervals during the day. The game required him to maintain a running total, adding the numbers 1 to 9.

Heidi was quiet in class and tended only to offer comment when asked directly. She was studious in her approach to work and made steady progress in English and mathematics. Heidi's technical ability in reading was good as was her comprehension, but she read aloud in monotone with no expression. The teacher decided to engage in shared reading with Heidi, using a text where conversation played a dominant role.

Ricky had a lively sense of humour but was not making progress in reading. He pointed to each word in turn as he read, breaking words down phonetically. He appeared not to use the small illustrations on the page to help decode new vocabulary and could not answer questions about the text after reading a passage aloud. The teacher found a new series of books for Ricky to read. The books had a small number of words on each page with an illustration on the facing page. They were short and included humourous characters.

Angela worked at speed in everything she did and was usually the first to finish. Her work was seldom of a good standard and regularly needed to be adjusted or corrected. The teacher worked with Angela to develop a small number of items for her to check before a piece of work could be considered as complete. As Angela became familiar with this approach new items were added to her personal checklist

Figure 1.1 The learning needs of four pupils in a Y3 class

1.3 What are the planning and assessment cycles?

The planning cycle (Figure 1.2) is the process by which teachers address pupils' learning needs. The four stages of the planning cycle are evident within the pupil descriptions of Figure 1.1. Firstly, the teacher monitors and assesses the present state of the pupils' learning, to determine which aspects of the curriculum are most relevant to their learning needs and how these should be taught. Secondly, the teacher plans a new learning experience by developing appropriate learning objectives and activities and deciding how pupils' learning is likely to be evidenced. Thirdly, she puts this into action by teaching. The teacher may at this stage decide to alter her original plan due to assessment she makes while teaching. If, for example, she discovers that pupils are unfamiliar with vocabulary she had assumed they understood the teacher may decide to use different words.

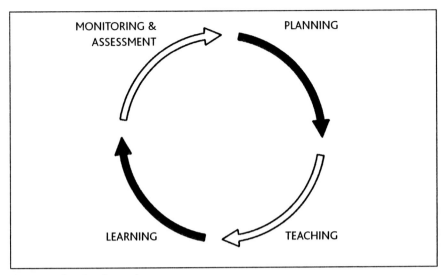

Figure 1.2 The planning cycle

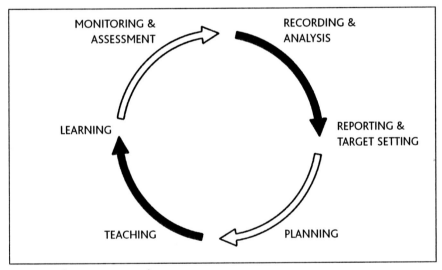

Figure 1.3 The assessment cycle

This, fourthly, enables the pupils to learn. The teacher then assesses pupils' learning in order to plan for the next stage in the cycle. With each revolution of the planning cycle the teacher becomes more familiar with the pupils' learning needs and is able to make plans which are increasingly matched to their needs. The planning cycle is formative as it informs future teaching and learning.

The assessment cycle (Figure 1.3) provides greater detail by extending the planning cycle and relating it to more formalised practice. The assessments made by the teacher are, where appropriate, recorded. The records are analysed and form the basis of reporting and target setting with pupils, parents or other teaching professionals. The targets are then built into future plans which inform teaching and learning. The assessment cycle is formative but may be summative, providing a summation of learning at a given point, for example, when statutory assessment has been undertaken.

1.4 What is statutory assessment?

Statutory assessment is assessment that must be undertaken by law. The Foundation Stage Profile is an assessment that takes place as pupils begin their school careers and is based upon the Early Learning Goals of the Foundation Stage (QCA 1999a www.qca.org.uk/ca/foundation). The End of Key Stage 1 and Key Stage 2 assessment is based upon the Attainment Targets of the National Curriculum (www.nc.uk.net) and is described numerically using 'levels'. Parents receive details of statutory assessments in relation to their own children through oral and written reports.

A wider audience can access details of the percentages of pupils at each National Curriculum level through the Governors' Annual Report to Parents and Office for Standards in Education (OFSTED) inspection reports of individual schools. Primary Performance Tables are also published for Key Stage 2, focusing solely on results in the core subjects of English, mathematics and science, not the formative and diagnostic work undertaken regularly to improve the learning of individual pupils across the curriculum.

1.5 Who is involved in MARRA?

Beyond the classroom MARRA involves a range of individuals and organisations including the Department for Education and Skills (DfES), which encompasses the Qualifications and Curriculum Authority (QCA), test development and marking agencies, LEA advisory and psychological services, the school governing body, the head teacher and teaching staff. The roles of individuals and organisations are wide-ranging, from writing test questions for the use of all 11 year olds across the country, to assessing the needs of an individual pupil through an IEP.

Within the classroom the teacher has a leading role in MARRA, assisted by Learning Support Assistants (LSAs) and visiting professionals and supported by the expertise and advice of other teachers. Teachers work within the time constraints of the school day and individual lessons, particularly in literacy and numeracy lessons which follow the formats and subdivisions of those recommended in the National Literacy Strategy (NLS) and National Numeracy Strategy (NNS) (DfEE 1998b; 1999a). Classes are diverse in their pupil make-up and may include a range of abilities, needs and social and cultural backgrounds. Pressures to develop curriculum areas are never far away as knowledge and technology grow together. Amid all of this, the teacher must focus upon the learning needs of pupils, to ascertain what they know, understand and can do and to provide effective and appropriate learning experiences. MARRA should not be seen as an addition to teaching and learning but as an essential part of it.

Similarly pupils should be encouraged to take a significant role in monitoring, assessment, recording, reporting and accountability to enable them to grow as learners. Learning how to learn, metacognition, requires pupils to become actively involved in the learning process, to be aware of their learning strategies and thinking processes (Nisbet and Shucksmith 1986; Fisher 1990), rather than simply being passive recipients of teaching. Pupils can engage in this process with the help and guidance of the teacher through their cognitive, affective and conative responses, which focus upon knowledge, emotion and motivation respectively.

1.6 MARRA: meeting the standards

The aim of this book is to enable trainee teachers and NQTs, whose classroom experience is necessarily limited, to link the theory and practice of MARRA both to meet the standards and to enhance their professional practice. The main chapters focus upon Monitoring, Assessment, Recording, Reporting and Accountability, building one upon the next to introduce terminology, issues and strategies. The book provides an analysis of each aspect of MARRA and gives references throughout the text to encourage readers to explore specific issues in greater depth through a range of literature, from the education press to academic journals and texts.

To gain the most from the text readers should work through the activities, discussions and case study questions contained in each of the main chapters. The activities, some of which are school based, develop theoretical and practical understanding. The discussion points encourage readers to reflect upon and question issues of theory and practice in MARRA. The case studies describe real situations in each area of MARRA. The questions which follow them raise areas for further debate and consideration and model the types of questions which students and NQTs should ask when engaging with MARRA in taught courses and in school-based work. Some of the activities, discussion points and case studies can be used by individuals but they will become more meaningful if used with one, two or more colleagues, within a group tutorial, seminar, in-service training (INSET) session or staff meeting. Such interaction provides a greater range of experience, with each colleague multiplying the number of school situations in the discussion and bringing a variety of views and insights into MARRA. The recording sheets, given in the appendices, have been tried, tested and developed in schools by trainees and teachers. They offer a starting point for practice which can be adjusted to suit personal and professional needs. A glossary of terms is provided for quick reference.

Note: Names of schools, teachers, students and pupils have been altered to maintain anonymity. To avoid the awkwardness of using he/she, individual teachers are identified as 'she' and individual pupils as 'he'.

CHAPTER 2

Monitoring

The National Curriculum is part of the 1988 Education Reform Act. The Act aims to ensure that schools teach a balanced range of subjects, set clear objectives, and monitor each pupil's learning.

(SEAC 1990a)

2.1 What is monitoring?

The dictionary defines monitoring as 'maintaining regular surveillance on a situation' (Cassell 1998). Traditionally it has been said that good teachers have 'eyes in the back of their heads'. While this idea has been the source of amusement to many a pupil it has credence too, as monitoring requires the teacher to be aware of all that is happening in the classroom. Kounin (1970) labelled this 'withitness', a skill which every effective practitioner needs to develop.

In a classroom context, monitoring is the skill of being able to have a constant, clear and accurate overview of pupils within a learning situation and environment. Teachers have a responsibility for the children in their care which is both legal and moral. The health and safety of some 30 individuals within a given space is clearly an important consideration, but so too is the social, physical, emotional and educational growth of the children.

Effective teachers are aware of and react to their pupils as a class and as individuals. They know what the pupils should be doing, when they should be doing it, why they should be doing it and with whom. Teachers observe and listen constantly. They analyse. They make decisions and act upon them. Kounin indicated that pupils are aware of and react to their teacher's 'withitness'. Yet all this takes place so frequently and at such pace it is barely discernible to the untrained observer.

By monitoring, the teacher can look for patterns and changes to patterns of attainment, approach or attitude. Where necessary the teacher can decide to undertake further detailed assessments with one or more pupils or assess the learning of many against one learning objective. The use of monitoring and assessment together can help determine pupils' needs and enhance their future learning experiences.

As with many skills, some people have a greater aptitude than others who have to practise and develop their abilities. Wragg (1984) indicated the nature of the task which teachers face when working with a class of pupils, by drawing upon a range of previous studies.

> Teachers may have up to 200 days a year with their classes, and various studies have shown over 1,000 interpersonal exchanges in a day (Jackson 1962), teachers asking on average 348 questions a day (Floyd 1960), some in inner-city schools spending up to 75 per cent of their time trying to keep order (Deutch 1960), or teachers allowing on average one second between a pupil answer and their own next statement
>
> (Rowe 1972) (p. 10)

Although there have been changes in the curriculum and its delivery since these studies, the essential nature of the teachers' task remains unaltered. There are few who could hold in their heads, with accuracy, all the information and decision-making of each day, but there are many more who could plan, observe, analyse, make decisions and write notes to remind themselves of any significant actions. A clarity of purpose, alongside systems and structures, enables effective monitoring of learning in the classroom.

In a school context, professional monitoring systems exist in parallel with the monitoring of learning in the classroom (Tymms 1999; Clarke 2001). The purpose of such systems is to oversee the provision of appropriate teaching, learning and assessment within the school as a whole. Teachers who are year or subject coordinators and members of the senior management team regularly monitor these areas by discussing progress with individuals and groups of teachers, examining records and observing teaching. The constant, clear and accurate overview enables the provision of additional support, resources and advice when necessary.

2.2 What should be monitored and why?

While the monitoring of learning is paramount, it cannot be seen in complete isolation from pupils' growth in other directions. Indeed the 1988 Education Reform Act which introduced the National Curriculum and its assessment, was intended 'to promote the balanced spiritual, moral, cultural, mental and physical development of pupils and prepare them for adult life'. Pupils' social interactions and their physical and emotional well-being necessarily impinge upon their learning. Teachers need to recognise these and any other contributory influences and monitor them accordingly. A pupil's underachievement may be due to social, physical or emotional factors, rather than a lack of understanding. For example, a pupil who is being teased for being overweight, or is displaying reduced concentration through loss of hearing, or is getting used to having a new baby in the family could also display underachievement. Teachers should be sensitive to pupils' needs and help them to develop by recognising them as complex individuals as well as learners.

The monitoring of learning should not be an end in itself but should result in action if and when necessary, to enable pupils to make progress in their learning. For this reason the teacher should know what the pupils are to learn, *the learning objective*, and how this is likely to manifest itself, *the evidence of attainment*. The teacher should also be able to identify what the pupil actually learns, *the learning outcome*. If the learning objective and the evidence of attainment have been considered at the planning stage, the teacher is better placed to determine whether learning has occurred and how the learning of individuals or groups or the class differs from her expectation. The monitoring of learning is purposeful if the teacher then analyses any variations from the norm and takes appropriate action, such as an alteration to the direction or intensity of the teaching or learning. Each of these points is now considered in greater detail.

2.3 What is a learning objective?

A learning objective is a brief statement of what pupils should have learnt by the end of a given period of time, usually a lesson. Learning objectives should be clear, focused and achievable. Newby (1996, p. 43) states that 'Good learning objectives are matched to the learner's abilities. They thus evidence the teacher's awareness of the child as an individual.' If teachers know what they want pupils to learn, monitoring becomes easier. If other adults in the classroom know the learning objectives they can share in this role. If pupils know the learning objectives they can monitor their own learning with greater understanding.

Three common difficulties in writing learning objectives are to confuse them with aims, activities or teaching objectives. Learning objectives are not aims. Aims are long term and more global in their coverage. Learning objectives are the small steps towards an aim. Learning objectives are not activities. Activities give details of what is going to happen in the lesson and what the pupils are expected to do. Learning objectives identify what pupils are to learn by the end of the lesson. Learning objectives are not teaching objectives. Teaching objectives focus upon the teacher's actions. Learning objectives focus upon the pupils' learning.

✎ ACTIVITY 2.1

Use the four categories of learning objectives, aims, activities and teaching objectives to sort the following 10 statements. Compare your results with a colleague and discuss your reasoning.

- To understand multiplication
- To record a composition
- To practise rolling, jumping and balancing
- To compare everyday materials
- To learn about colour
- To organise historical information
- To complete a worksheet about quadrilaterals
- To select appropriate materials
- To introduce new instruments
- To read fluently

✎ ACTIVITY 2.2

Examine the objectives set out in the National Literacy and National Numeracy Strategies. Are they learning objectives or teaching objectives? Give reasons for your answers.

2.4 Who determines the learning objectives?

Teachers write learning objectives in their lesson plans. This suggests that the learning objectives are decided upon and developed by the teacher alone, but pupils also have a role to play. Pollard (2002) discussed three different 'learning processes' prevalent in recent years: behaviourism, constructivism and social constructivism. Within each of these the instigator of the learning objectives varies.

Behaviourist learning objectives are conceived by the teacher who knows what she wants the pupils to learn. The pupils have no role in determining what they wish to learn but are passive receivers of the teacher's decision-making. The learning objectives focus upon specific skills or particular aspects of knowledge, with the teacher interpreting the curriculum. The learning could be in complete isolation from the pupils' past experiences and understanding.

In stark contrast to behaviourism, constructivist approaches require the pupils to take a leading role in 'the selection, pacing and evaluation' of their work (Pollard 2002, p. 140). This could mean 30 pupils in a class each devising learning objectives and individual programmes of work according to their personal experiences and understanding. The teacher's role is one of facilitator and the curriculum develops according to interest rather than prescription.

Social constructivism recognises the need for some structure and some flexibility. Teachers and pupils negotiate and share learning objectives using source material, such as a structured curriculum, in conjunction with personal needs and interests. The teacher's role is to scaffold learning, to help the pupil to make connections with and to further their experience and understanding.

Discussion 2.1

The National Literacy and National Numeracy Strategies have given objectives which provide progression through the subject. Teachers are expected to determine which objectives are appropriate to their pupils and to share these with them. To what extent do the objectives of the National Literacy and National Numeracy Strategies follow behaviourist, constructivist or social constructivist models of learning?

2.5 What is evidence of attainment?

The phrase 'evidence of attainment' was used in the original End of Key Stage 1 Standard Assessment Tasks (SATs) in 1991. The phrase 'what to look for' was also used to give clarification.

Evidence of attainment concerns fact not speculation. However, deciding upon evidence of attainment is less clear cut. There are two questions to consider when looking for evidence of attainment in the classroom. Firstly, how and when does learning manifest itself? For example, what will pupils need to do, say, write or make to show they have attained a particular learning objective? Is evidence of attainment more likely to be seen in a final product, such as a piece of writing, or within the process of the pupils' working, such as when they discuss how to tackle a mathematics investigation? Secondly, can all aspects of learning be evidenced? For example, what evidence of attainment would be needed to demonstrate art or music appreciation?

> **Discussion 2.2**
>
> '...curriculum theory which views educational objectives as standards by which to measure educational achievement overlooks those modes of achievement incapable of measurement.'
>
> (Eisner 1985, p. 35)
>
> To which areas of the curriculum might Eisner be referring? What differences would there be in monitoring cognitive, affective or conative areas of learning?

Evidence of attainment is often sought in relation to pupils' *knowledge, skills and understanding*. But these areas are very broad and refer to long-term aims rather than short-term objectives and consequently cannot be easily identified in the classroom.

The behaviourist learning model suggests that 'knowledge' and 'skills' can be broken down into suitable learning objectives which pupils will or will not be able to demonstrate, for example, 'to know the six times table' or 'to use capital letters and full stops to define a sentence'. But Newby (1996, p. 43) states '...it is quite unacceptable to regard learning only in terms of progression from one highly specific objective to another...teachers...will lose sight of the intrinsic value of learning'.

This was evident in 1862, long before the conception of the National Curriculum, when the Revised Code was put into place through the legislation which followed the Newcastle Report of 1861. Her Majesty's Inspectors (HMIs) were required to monitor the educational provision within a school by questioning pupils on their knowledge and skills relating to six 'Standards' in reading, writing and arithmetic, two of which are given in Table 2.1.

Table 2.1 Standards I and VI of the Revised Code (Maclure 1968)

	Standard I	Standard VI
Reading	Narrate in monosyllables.	A short ordinary paragraph in a newspaper, or another modern narrative
Writing	Form on blackboard or slate, from dictation, letters, capital and small manuscript.	Another short ordinary paragraph in a newspaper, or another modern narrative, slowly dictated once by a few words at a time.
Arithmetic	Form on blackboard or slate, from dictation, figures up to 20; name at sight figures up to 20; add and subtract figures up to 10, orally, from examples on blackboard.	A sum in practice or bills of parcels.

Were HMIs testing 'knowledge' and 'skills' or factual recall and the ability to replicate? Was 'understanding' of any importance? The nature of the monitoring of pupils' abilities and the 'payment by results' which followed, not surprisingly led to a narrowing of the curriculum towards reading, writing and arithmetic.

If knowledge is more than knowing facts, how is it possible to tell whether pupils 'know' something or are just remembering what they have been told on another occasion? Similarly, if a 'skill' is simply the ability to do something well in a particular context, should pupils also be able to make decisions about where and when it should be applied? To what extent does 'understanding' apply to the learning of knowledge and skills?

'Understanding' cannot be described in precise behaviourist terms. It rests far more with constructivist and social constructivist models where the pupils' contribution is essential if connections are to be made with the pupils' previous experiences and understanding. Understanding is not easily witnessed by an observer.

In a classroom context the distinction between understanding and the ability to reach a correct answer by following a taught procedure, may not be immediately apparent. For example, it is possible for two pupils both to achieve full marks for a mathematics exercise, one through understanding of the mathematics involved and how it connects to other areas of the subject, the other through the use of methods learned and practised. Skemp (1989, p. 2) referred to these two levels of understanding as 'relational' and 'instrumental'. He stated that relational understanding was 'knowing what to do and why' while instrumental understanding was no more than 'rules without reason'.

To monitor understanding the teacher needs to discuss work with pupils in order to discover whether correct connections are being made. To ascertain the evidence of attainment the teacher necessarily needs to monitor the process of the pupils' work, not just the product, by asking pupils appropriate and well phrased questions. Kyriacou's (1995) term for this was 'active probing'. Questions should encourage pupils to demonstrate their understanding. Questions are therefore more likely to be open rather than closed or leading and the teacher should provide sufficient 'wait time' (Wood 1988) to enable pupils to consider connections and formulate an answer.

2.6 What is a learning outcome?

A learning outcome is the learning that has actually taken place. Often the learning outcome will be the same as the learning objective, and be demonstrated through the evidence of attainment. But there are two main reasons why the learning outcome might differ from the anticipated evidence of attainment. Firstly, the pupil may not meet the learning objective because of inaccurate or inappropriate matching of work to the pupil's needs and abilities. Secondly, the teacher may not have considered the range of potential learning outcomes. For example, in a lesson about written multiplication algorithms the pupil may simply confuse two different methods and demonstrate a lack of understanding of the task itself or he may use a suitable method which is unfamiliar to and not anticipated by the teacher.

The teacher should monitor occasions when the learning outcome does not meet the learning objective for the class or groups or individuals. Such monitoring, when analysed, can provide an insight into the teaching and learning which is taking place. The Subject Monitoring Sheet for English (Figure 2.1) provides an example of this. The learning of a group of pupils was monitored for a week against learning objectives drawn from the National Literacy Strategy. The monitoring was coded as follows:

S   significant strengths shown

✔   learning objective = learning outcome

W   significant weaknesses shown

☐   insufficient evidence to make judgement

A   absent

An analysis of the completed monitoring sheet suggests that, as most pupils had difficulty with LO3, the level of work or its teaching may have been at fault. The level of Amber's work may need to be reviewed to decide whether it is sufficiently challenging, whereas Luke is just coping and Jake has missed most of the work undertaken during the week and will need additional support on his return to school.

There are other learning outcomes of which the teacher should be aware. They relate to the hidden curriculum. Pollard (2002, p. 67) defined the hidden curriculum as 'what is "picked up" about such things as the role of the teacher and the role of the learner, about the status and relationships of each, about attitudes towards learning and to school'. For example, pupils may learn that 'having a go' is more important to a teacher than waiting to be sure of a correct answer, or they may learn only to answer questions when accuracy is guaranteed as incorrect answers will be ridiculed by their peers. The hidden curriculum encompasses attitudes and approaches and needs to be monitored as it too impinges on the pupils' learning.

2.7 What are the implications of monitoring for classroom practice?

There are several implications for classroom practice. Monitoring requires visibility so it is useful to move around the classroom to determine the positions

SUBJECT MONITORING SHEET

Subject: English NLS (Text, Word and Sentence level)

Learning Objective	LO1: To prepare a play script T	LO2: To take account of exclamation marks when reading dialogue S	LO3: To recognise how spellings of verbs alter when adding 'ing' W	LO4: To recognise key differences of text layout between prose and play scripts T	LO5: To take account of commas to mark pauses when reading aloud S
Date	1st October	2nd October	3rd October	4th October	6th October
Ashleigh	✓		W	✓	
LeeAnna	✓	S	W	✓	A
Jake	A	A	A	A	✓
Brendan	✓		W	✓	
Luke	W	✓	W	✓	W
Amber	✓	✓	✓	✓	✓
Notes			Teaching target: to look at different groups of words when adding 'ing'		

Figure 2.1 Subject monitoring sheet for English

at which all pupils can be seen and to identify where visibility is restricted. There may be areas in or beyond the room where pupils can work comfortably but cannot be seen. The teacher should decide whether to ask an LSA or parent helper to monitor the pupils if she is unable to do so.

Moving around the classroom during the lesson provides a useful monitoring opportunity. More can be gained from it if the 'ripple effect' (Kounin 1970) is used to advantage. Kounin describes the 'ripple effect' as the effect which a reprimand, or desist, can have on others in the classroom. Although Kounin's work focused upon discipline, a similar effect occurs if a teacher talks to an individual within a group or classroom area about the quality of his work. Quite quickly the message that the teacher is looking for interesting characterisation in a story, or accurate measuring of angles when drawing nets, spreads around pupils close by when she praises the achievement of an individual.

Marking is a useful tool for monitoring pupils' learning (see Chapter 5, section 5.6). The effect of marking in the classroom when pupils are working on the task is twofold. Firstly, it provides both the pupil and the teacher with an indication of learning within the context of the work set and adjustments can be made formatively by the teacher and the learner. Secondly, it enables the teacher to gain an overview of the pupils' work, and bring the class together if necessary, for further teaching. A useful strategy is to mark the work of one or two pupils in each group or area of the room and to give them oral support for their learning. The 'ripple effect' will make sure the message is spread as the teacher moves to another group. By sampling the work of six carefully chosen individuals who represent a spread of ability in the class, the teacher can monitor the learning of many and reiterate or develop a teaching point, before continuing to mark the work of others in the class.

When planning how to monitor the pupils' learning it is important to decide upon a recording mechanism which suits the purpose and the teacher as an individual. The monitoring sheet in Figure 2.1 provides an example of a sheet which enables monitoring of several related events and is simple to administer. There should be an indication on a monitoring sheet of to what, to whom and to when it refers, enabling cross referencing to a lesson plan.

Analysis of a monitoring sheet becomes more evident after several sessions, when patterns occur. The teacher needs to recognise what the monitoring tells her about the learning of individuals, groups and the class as a whole. For example, she may notice that a particular pupil's work has been erratic and consider whether it is due to factors within or beyond school. She may choose to talk to an individual about his own perception of the work and whether he would benefit from the move to a different ability group. The teacher also needs to recognise what monitoring tells her about the teaching which took place. The teacher may decide to pitch her work with the class at a higher or lower level or try a different way to approach the subject. An essential feature of monitoring is the teacher's willingness to use it flexibly to help pupils to make progress in their learning.

Most importantly though, if monitoring of pupils' learning is to be effective all those involved, both adults and children, need to know the learning objectives of the lesson. The teacher should consider how the learning might be demonstrated through evidence of attainment and share this, along with questions to elicit pupils' understanding, with other adults.

2.8 How can other adults be involved in monitoring?

Everyone in the classroom can be involved in monitoring learning, both adults and pupils, but the major role is necessarily played by the teacher, who has responsibility for the pupils' development.

An increasing number of primary school classes have Learning Support Assistants assigned to them. The use of LSAs began in early years settings and through the allocation of funding for the personal support of pupils with a statement of special educational need (Moyles and Suschitzky 1997; Thomas 1992). By 1997, 24,000 were employed (DfEE 1997a) and the figure rose further with funding for the National Literacy and Numeracy initiatives. Designated courses for LSAs provided training in the support of English, mathematics and special educational needs, but the roles of LSAs in schools have varied greatly according to the need of the school and the attitude of teachers towards para-professionals (Bryan and Headington 1998).

The title of Teacher Assistant has reflected the development of the LSA's role. Standards for Higher Level Teacher Assistants (DfES 2003) will establish the role further as numbers move towards 200,000.

Assistants provide teachers with 'extra hands and extra eyes' (McGarvey et al. 1996). When this is coupled with an awareness and understanding of shared learning objectives, through discussion and training, assistants can play a role in monitoring pupils' learning. For example, during whole-class introductions and conclusions of lessons, the assistant could note for the teacher which pupils needed additional guidance in answering questions based upon the learning objective. During group activities the assistant could note which pupils demonstrated confidence in their approach and attitude towards the learning objective.

Parent helpers are often found in primary school classrooms. They necessarily come from all walks of life, some with training, some without, but all with an interest in the development of the pupils. With guidance from the teacher, parent helpers can also provide support in monitoring specific aspects of the pupils' learning.

2.9 How can pupils be involved in monitoring?

Pupils should be encouraged to monitor their own learning and become more aware of themselves as learners. Nisbet and Shucksmith (1986, p. 28) saw pupils' monitoring as a 'continuous attempt to match efforts, answers and discoveries to initial questions or purposes'.

For this to be achieved the learning objectives must be shared or negotiated with the pupils in language they will understand (Clarke 2001). Negotiated learning objectives may have developed from a previous learning experience and targets. For example, if during an investigative mathematics activity it became evident that pupils were not familiar with factors and multiples, the teacher and pupils may agree to look at these in more detail the following day before tackling similar investigations.

Discussion 2.3

'...although teachers are very good at telling children what to do, they very rarely tell them why they are doing it...'

(Bennett 1994, p. 45)

Does this statement reflect your experience? What are the benefits of sharing and negotiating learning objectives with pupils?

The teacher should share learning objectives with the pupils at the beginning of the lesson and revisit them at the end of the lesson when she should help the pupils to identify what and how they have learned. She should indicate any mini-targets which have been developed and achieved during the lesson, such as a pupil explaining how he used a dictionary when he didn't know the meaning of a word, and encourage pupils to share their strategies for learning. The teacher should also encourage pupils to consider areas which they need to develop and so negotiate new learning objectives.

This approach requires pupil–teacher interaction and strongly demonstrates the social-constructivist model of working across the 'zone of proximal development' (Vygotsky 1978). It also builds upon the notion that personal involvement is a key to learning. As Fisher (1990, p. 114) stated, 'We remember best when what we need to remember:

- is important for us
- has some personal relevance
- is meaningful in itself
- can be connected to something we already know

- is of immediate use
- is of manageable size
- is repeated and strengthened through repetition'.

2.10 Case studies in monitoring

CASE STUDY 2.1

Mandy was in the first year of a BA QTS degree. She was on the final week of a three week block practice in a large urban infant school with a class of 25 Year R children.

Mandy collected the children from the playground. She brought them into the classroom and told them to sit in the carpeted area. After several noisy minutes the children settled and Mandy, who was sitting facing them, began to tell the children their tasks for the rest of the morning. The children were designated to four groups. The first was to work with the LSA on an art activity. The second was to work with a parent on a practical activity beyond the classroom. The third was to use the role play area. The fourth was to work with Mandy on a mathematics activity. Mandy told the children to move straight to their area of work. It took eight minutes before the children were in the appropriate areas.

At this point Mandy sat at the designated mathematics table in the middle of the room, with her back to the role play area and her side to the group working with the LSA. Before the lesson she had organised the table with counters and commercial scheme workbooks. Mandy told the children how to complete the next page of their workbooks. She did not use the counters. After her explanation she asked if the children understood. They nodded and she distributed the workbooks.

The children opened their books as Mandy moved away to talk to the group in the role play area, two of whom, she had now realised, were staging a fight with some swords. Mandy went to talk to the LSA and then moved back to the mathematics group. One child was working through the page steadily, using her fingers as a counting aid. Three were trying to help each other and the remaining two appeared to have drifted off task. Mandy sat down with the children and went through the task again with all of them, this time she demonstrated using the counters. Mandy asked the children if they understood. They nodded.

- What practical considerations should Mandy make to improve her monitoring skills?
- How could Mandy develop the pupils' metacognition?
- What targets would you set for Mandy if you were her tutor?

CASE STUDY 2.2

Gwyneth was a Year Two BEd student undertaking a four week block practice at a large rural 9–13 year middle school where pupils moved between subject specialist teachers. Gwyneth's timetable included mathematics, geography and pastoral responsibilities. The school had a traditional approach which was quite different to the primary school where she had successfully completed her first year block practice.

In Y6 mathematics, pupils completed exercises from a textbook or worksheet during the lessons and for homework. Gwyneth monitored the mathematics learning of pupils in Set Four (lowest ability with 18 pupils) by moving around the room, working with individuals, pairs and small groups, marking and keeping notes where appropriate. However, she found the same approach could not be used effectively with Set One (highest ability with 32 pupils) where the pupils worked more confidently and quickly, with fewer apparent difficulties. When Gwyneth collected the pupils' exercise books at the end of the lesson they were unable to use them for homework. She decided to mark the classwork and homework together, away from the pupils, when the exercise books were handed in the following day. As she marked the work Gwyneth found that she had not detected the errors made by some pupils in the lesson so their homework was also incorrect. They had practised making mistakes. Conversely some pupils had completed the work with no errors. Gwyneth could not tell whether the work was at the correct level or whether it was insufficiently challenging.

● What strategies could Gwyneth use to improve her monitoring of pupils' learning in Set One?

● What should Gwyneth do to determine whether the work which had been completed correctly was sufficiently demanding?

● Which areas of practice would you praise if you were her tutor? What practical considerations should Mandy make to improve her monitoring skills?

● How could Mandy develop the pupils' metacognition?

● What targets would you set for Mandy if you were her tutor?

CHAPTER 3

Assessment

Assessment does not stand outside teaching and learning but stands in dynamic interaction with it.

(Gipps 1996)

3.1 What is assessment?

Assessment was defined in the glossary of the Task Group for Assessment and Testing report as 'A general term enhancing all methods customarily used to appraise performance of an individual or group' (DES 1988). With such a broad definition it is not surprising that the term is often used to describe all aspects of MARRA. In this book, assessment refers to the work which teachers undertake to determine the learning and the learning needs of pupils. This includes the close examination of pupils' learning and learning practices and analysis of their learning needs. Assessment is more specific than monitoring. Where monitoring provides the teacher with an overview of the learning of many, assessment provides detailed information about the learning of one or more pupils within a few learning objectives, or of many pupils within one or more learning objectives (see Figure 3.1). Where monitoring provides the teacher with a constant overview of the learning of many (horizontal lines), assessment provides detailed information about the learning of one or more pupils within a few learning objectives, or of many pupils within one or more learning objectives (vertical lines).

This is more evident in a classroom situation when the teacher carries out a focused assessment with a group of pupils than it is when an End of Key Stage test is administered. With the former the teacher can observe, question and analyse responses to the activity, assessing both process and product, whereas with the latter only analysis of the product is possible. But in both cases the teacher assesses by analysing and drawing conclusions about a pupil's abilities, approaches and attitudes by drawing upon her previous experience with other pupils and her understanding of both the curriculum and the pupil's development.

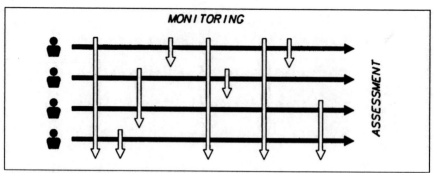

Figure 3.1 The links between monitoring and assessment

3.2 Why do teachers assess pupils' learning?

Assessment enables the teacher to determine the quality of pupils' learning. If the teacher knows this she can use assessment *for* learning by planning future learning experiences which will enhance pupils' learning experiences and by making connections with current knowledge, skills and understanding. She can use assessment formatively to develop teaching methods and approaches which will engage the pupils and make their work more meaningful.

Assessment *of* learning enables the school to provide information for others, including pupils, parents, other teaching professionals and the DfES, about the individual's progress in relation to his peers (see Chapter 5). The recipients can then draw conclusions from the summative information provided. As the recipients move further away from the individual pupil, the information given necessarily, and legally, becomes less qualitative and more quantitative. Assessments made by the teacher and through statutory tests are numbered according to levels defined in the National Curriculum Attainment Targets. These numbers enable comparison and provide opportunities for those working away from the school to determine the needs of the school and LEA (see Chapter 6).

The quantitative and summative nature of assessment *of* learning has often overshadowed the more qualitative and formative assessment *for* learning. But it has been recognised by practitioners and researchers alike that formative assessment provides a key vehicle for learning (Black and Wiliam 1998; Wiliam and Black 2002).

3.3 What should be assessed?

Assessment should focus upon *what* the pupil learns and *how* the pupil learns. The interrelationship between the two provides a rich source of data for the teacher in developing targets and future learning experiences for pupils and enables others to evaluate the content of the curriculum and the teaching methods employed.

Assessment of *what* pupils learn rests firmly upon the curriculum of the day. The curriculum defines the content of teaching, learning and assessment. As shown in Chapter 2, the Revised Code of 1862 emphasised teaching, learning and assessment of reading, writing and arithmetic. The National Curriculum has emphasised the core subjects of English (and Welsh for pupils in Wales), mathematics and science, the foundation subjects of information technology, history, geography, physical education, design technology, art and music, along with religious education, which had been a compulsory subject since the 1944 Education Act. The subject domain to be assessed was determined by the content of the National Curriculum and, in the case of religious education, agreed syllabuses. The statutory focus for assessment began with the core subjects. There were plans to assess many more areas of the curriculum, but these plans did not materialise due to the difficulties found in implementing a programme of national assessment which was deemed to be valid, reliable and manageable (Daugherty 1995).

Recent statutory assessment requirements dwell upon the core subjects but teachers assess pupils' learning in all aspects of the taught curriculum. Beyond the statutory testing arrangements there are no restrictions on how this is done although some LEAs require particular tests to be administered for a variety of purposes such as testing for selection at age 11.

Assessment of *how* pupils learn is left largely at the discretion of the teacher and the beliefs and values of the teacher and school. While some teachers may choose to assess the pupils' ability to work within a social and supported context, others may choose to assess pupils on their ability to work independently and without assistance. Some teachers may assess the pupils' ability to plan and organise their work, drawing upon a range of knowledge and skills, others may choose to assess pupils on their ability to structure their work within a given context. Learning often depends upon how curriculum areas are taught and this needs to be considered when assessing how pupils learn. If mathematics is always taught in a lively and interactive style and the pupils have been encouraged to learn through active engagement and questioning, is it appropriate to assess them through a formal and individualised written test?

In their research of primary classrooms, Torrance and Pryor (1998, p. 152) observed and identified 'two conceptually distinct approaches to classroom assessment' which they labelled as 'convergent' and 'divergent'. In the former the assessment demonstrates a constructivist view of learning and 'aims to discover *whether* the learner knows, understands or can do a predetermined thing'. In the latter the assessment demonstrates a behaviourist view of learning and 'aims to discover *what* the learner knows, understands or can do'. Torrance and Pryor also identified the practical implications of these two approaches, for example, in the different styles of questioning and the recording mechanisms used by the teacher.

✎ ACTIVITY 3.1

Working with several colleagues, list the approaches to assessment which you have witnessed being used by teachers in different schools and classrooms. Put them into the two groups of '*Whether* the learner knows' and 'What the learner knows'. Analyse and discuss your findings.

3.4 How are assessments referenced?

Assessments must be measured in relation to a scale or compared with another assessment of the same or a different pupil if they are to be understood. This is called referencing. Three types of referencing used frequently in primary education are criterion, ipsative and norm-referencing.

Assessments are frequently made by comparing the work of a pupil against set criteria. This enables the strengths and weaknesses of the pupil to be recognised and built upon. The criteria can be shared with the pupil who then knows what to do to succeed and when to ask for support.

Assessments judged against previous personal performance are ipsative-referenced. They enable the pupil to become more involved in the assessment process by reflecting upon past work and determining how it can be improved in the future. The teacher who builds upon this by developing pupils' metacognitive strategies can in turn lead the pupil to greater involvement in the learning and assessment process. Records of Achievement (RoAs) and Individual Pupil Portfolios provide an opportunity for teachers to develop ipsative-referenced assessment (see Chapter 4).

Norm-referencing follows a more traditional approach to assessment. Its purpose is to compare pupils with each other and the 'norm', to place pupils in rank order and show the spread of ability. In an assessment which is considered as valid and reliable, norm-referencing will distribute its sample across a normal curve of distribution. Unlike criterion and ipsative-referenced assessment, the purpose of norm-referenced assessment is not to 'generate specific information about what the individual child, knows, understands and can do' (Sutton 1991, p. 4), but to provide the same assessment for pupils of differing abilities and so highlight their differing abilities. It is not surprising that norm-referenced assessment has been used as a tool in the selection of pupils for entry into particular sets, streams or schools.

National Curriculum assessment was devised to provide criterion-referencing through criteria called Statements of Attainment (SoA). It has been suggested that the move from SoAs to Level Descriptions (LDs) following the Dearing Review (Dearing 1994) lost the intensity of TGAT's original recommendations for criterion-referencing (Shorrocks-Taylor 1999). But as Tymms (1999, p. 14) indicated '...norm- and criterion-referenced testing are rarely met in their pure forms and...much testing is a hybrid...when constructing the criteria for a criterion-referenced test norm-referencing is essential'. Was TGAT's original recommendation too 'pure' to be practical?

Discussion 3.1

Wiliam and Black (2002, p. 9) state that 'Assessment for learning is...intended to help pupils improve rather than rank ordering them or certifying their level of competence.' What referencing is most likely to support assessment *for* learning. Why?

3.5 What methods of assessment are there?

Assessment methods are as wide and varied as teaching methods. Some focus upon the end result of the pupils' work, the product, others on the work as it takes place, the process. Some require the pupil to work unaided, others require interaction with peers or an adult. Some are more costly in time and resources than others. Some are used within the statutory tests, others within Teacher Assessment. All methods of assessment require the teacher to have a clear understanding of the learning objectives and the evidence of attainment. All require the teacher to be objective, looking for factual evidence rather than making assumptions in a subjective manner. OFSTED (1998, p. 5) stated that 'In schools where teacher assessment has been used effectively to raise standards...teachers are proficient in using a range of assessment techniques in the classroom'. The general assessment methods of observation, questioning and testing are now considered in addition to the specific methods of running records, comprehension exercises and concept mapping.

A method of assessment used frequently by teachers is observation. The teacher can observe pupils working on practical and more formal written tasks. She can look at the methods pupils use and the approaches they take. The teacher can observe pupils' non-verbal communication to determine whether they are interested in the activity. She can observe pupils' interaction with their peers and listen to their comments. Observation focuses upon pupils' actions and interactions.

Discussion 3.2

Lee and Robert were Y3 pupils in an urban primary school. Lee enjoyed number work and was far beyond his peers in calculation skills. Robert had difficulties in reading. This had held him back in many areas, including mathematics, where he needed assistance in reading the instructions in workbooks. Lee and Robert were put in a group with two others for a 3-dimensional shape activity using connecting plastic straws to make pyramids and prisms. The teacher observed them from a distance.

The group immediately put Lee in a leading role whilst Robert sat back and appeared despondent. Lee began to plan how many straws were needed by trying to draw a pyramid on plain paper. He tried this several times and seemed to become frustrated. None of his drawings looked like a pyramid. Robert, quite independently, played with some of the straws and connectors. He joined them together and made a square. He looked satisfied with this and made another. Robert held the two squares in his hands and moved them a little away from each other. He examined them for a while before picking out four more straws to connect the squares together. Robert had made a cube.

What assessment of Lee and Robert can be made from this observation?
How objective is the account of the observation?

Observation in its purest form requires the teacher to be a passive onlooker to a situation, without interjection or comment. Even a facial expression may be seized upon by a pupil looking for feedback from the teacher. It is not surprising then that such observation is difficult to achieve in a classroom, which is a naturally social environment where the teacher actively engages with pupils' learning. And while observation provides evidence of the pupils' actions and interactions, it can only provide evidence of their rationale and reasoning if this is verbalised or written. To gain access to information on the latter, questioning is essential. Questioning enlivens observation. It enables the teacher to delve into pupils' thinking and assess in greater detail than observation alone. A teacher may observe a pupil selecting a reading book from several others on the shelf, but only his answer to the question 'Why did you choose it?' will indicate whether he was keen to read more books by a particular author or that he chose it because it looked easier than the others.

Questioning is a key skill for all teachers but, as Brown and Wragg (1993, p. 3) indicate 'Our reasons for asking questions of children are rather different from those in everyday conversation...We often ask questions of children, not to obtain new knowledge for ourselves but to find out what the children already know.' Questions help the teacher to teach and to assess. A skilled teacher can develop pupils' thinking by asking searching questions which require them to bring together many facets of their experience. Similarly she may ask a question to check whether or not a particular fact is known. Different types of questions elicit different types of responses and so serve different purposes. A closed question such as 'What is 6 x 7?' provides only one correct response, whereas an open question such as 'Why did Anne Frank write a diary?' encourages a range of responses which will demonstrate different levels of thinking.

Not all questions are effective aids to assessment. Questions such as 'Would it be better to start with a plan?' suggest the direction of the answer and are no more than teacher instructions. A teacher with a fixed goal in mind may involve pupils in playing a 'guessing game' rather than encouraging them to think about the problem for themselves (Torrance and Pryor 1998). Assessment is then limited to the pupils' ability to carry out the teacher's instructions.

As indicated in Chapter 2, section 2.5, the teacher also needs to provide sufficient time for the pupil to consider the question and 'respond in more extended and thoughtful ways' (Fisher 1990, p. 17). The research of Askew and Wiliam (1995) suggested that, in a mathematics context, a suitable 'wait time' was three seconds.

When planning for assessment it is important to consider how questions will be asked and, if possible, to rehearse them with a colleague to determine whether they will elicit the responses anticipated. It is also important to consider when to ask questions, whether before, during or after an activity. Initial questions, intervention questions and review questions all enable the teacher to assess the pupils' understanding. Figure 3.2 provides an example of question planning undertaken by a teacher assessing pupils' abilities in using and applying mathematics through an activity based upon the story 'The Doorbell Rang' by Pat Hutchins.

Initial question	How many ways can Grandma's cookies be shared?
Intervention questions	What resources will help you?
	What do you need to do first?
	How will you record that?
	Can you tell us what you did and why you did it?
	What are you doing?
	Why are you doing that?
	What have you discovered?
	What will you do now?
	Was there a better way of doing it?
	What would happen if...?
Review questions	Has everyone reached the same results?
	Why has this happened?

Figure 3.2 Questions (adapted from Buckinghamshire LEA 1993)

Re-read the observation account in Discussion 3.2. List the questions you would ask Lee and Robert before, during and after the 3-dimensional shape activity, to assess their rationale and reasoning.

Some assessment methods tend to be used more frequently in one subject rather than another. The traditional examples of these, which are still used regularly in many schools, are spelling and mental arithmetic tests. Pupils may be provided with information to learn at the beginning of the week and given an oral test at the end of the week. Graded spelling and mental arithmetic books provide a progression in the level of work encountered, sometimes providing contextualised questions such as 'If Mary had five sweets and Peter gave her three more, how many sweets would Mary have?', in addition to context-free questions such as '15 − 7 = '. Although such tests provide the teacher with some indication of the pupils' abilities to learn and recall factual information, formative and diagnostic assessment can only come from closer analysis of a pupil's work. Mark's spelling test result is 5/10 (see Figure 3.3). His difficulty stems from the use of 'ie' rather than 'ei' in certain words but this would not be evident to a teacher who simply collected the scores.

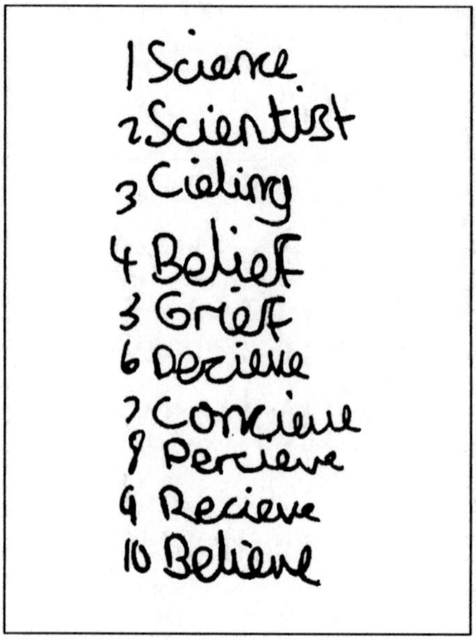

1 Science.
2 Scientist
3 Cieling
4 Belief
5 Grief
6 Decieve
7 Concieve
8 Percieve
9 Recieve
10 Believe

Figure 3.3 Mark's spelling test

Similarly an assessment which ascertains pupils' mental arithmetic methods may be more advantageous than simply assessing their ability to give correct answers (Figure 3.4).

NAME: Anna

Calculation	=	How I know
10 + 11	21	10+10 + 1 = 21
12 + 13	25	12 + 12 = 24 + 1 = 25
15 + 16	31	15 + 15 + 1 = 31
19 + 18	37	20 + 18 = 38 − 1 = 37
21 + 19	40	21 − 1 + 1 to 19 = 20 20 + 20 = 40
24 + 23	47	24 + 24 = 48 − 1 = 47
27 + 30	57	30 + 30 = 60 − 3 = 57

Figure 3.4 Anna's calculations

A subject specific assessment which has gained in popularity since its use in the Key Stage 1 tests, is the running record (Clay 1993), an observation survey and version of miscue analysis which is used in guided reading to help the teacher to diagnose pupils' difficulties. The pupil reads aloud to the teacher from a book. After a few pages the teacher begins to record, on a separate sheet containing the same text, the errors and approaches used by the pupil during a predetermined passage. The teacher uses a code to indicate strengths and weaknesses in key points of reading development. The teacher can then analyse the sheet to determine whether the pupil reads for meaning, recognises structure and syntax and uses visual information in addition to his ability to self-monitor, search and self-correct (Figure 3.5).

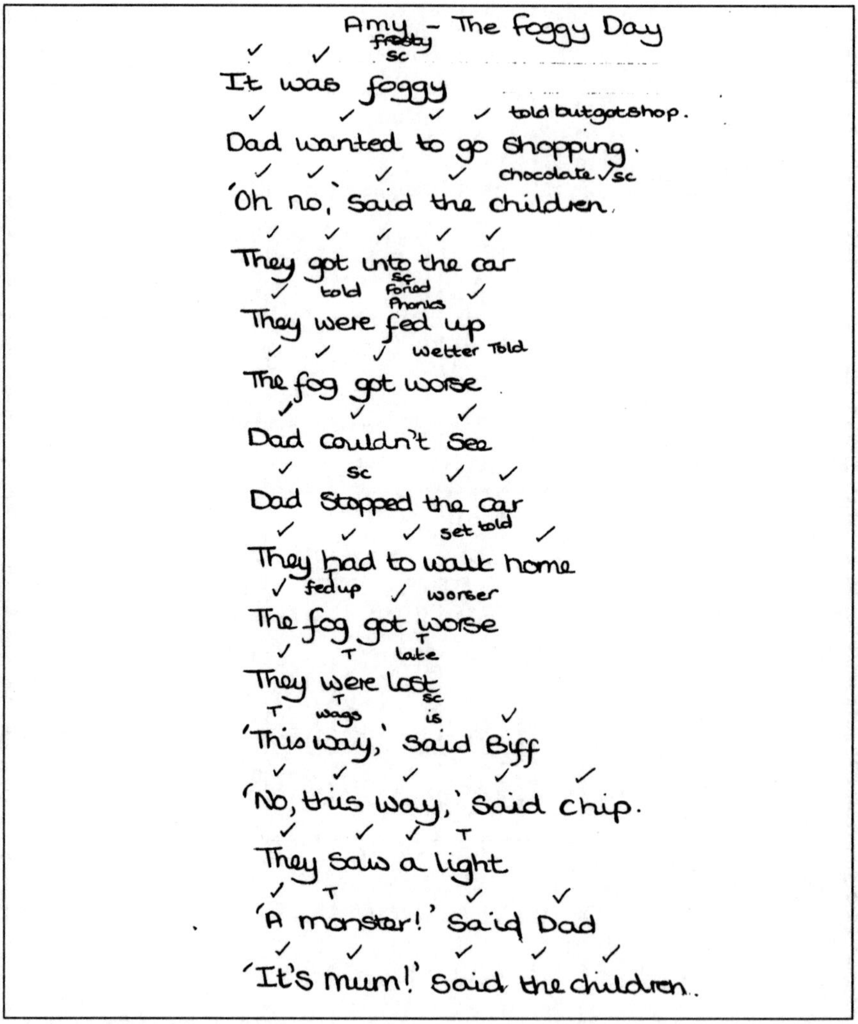

Amy – The Foggy Day
froggy *sc*
✓ ✓
It was foggy
✓ ✓ ✓ ✓ *told butgotshop.*
Dad wanted to go shopping.
✓ ✓ ✓ ✓ *chocolate ✓sc*
'Oh no,' said the children.
✓ ✓ ✓ ✓ ✓
They got into the car
✓ *told* *sc foried Phonics* ✓
They were fed up
✓ ✓ ✓ *wetter Told*
The fog got worse.
✓ ✓ ✓
Dad couldn't see
✓ *sc* ✓ ✓
Dad stopped the car
✓ ✓ ✓ *set told* ✓
They had to walk home
✓ *fedup* ✓ *worser*
The fog got worse
✓ *T late*
They were lost
T wags is ✓
'This way,' said Biff
✓ ✓ ✓ ✓ ✓
'No, this way,' said chip.
✓ ✓ ✓ *T*
They saw a light
✓ *T* ✓ ✓
'A monster!' said Dad
✓ ✓ ✓ ✓
'It's mum!' said the children.

Figure 3.5 Amy's running record

Fountas and Pinnell (1996) questioned the traditional assessment of comprehension through formal methods, where the pupil reads a given passage and answers questions relating to it, and commented that, 'Because comprehension is a complex and invisible process, it is easy to confuse methods designed to get evidence of comprehension with comprehension itself.' If, for example, a pupil uses a formulaic approach, using the words in the question to search for a sentence in the text then simply combining the two to give an answer, rather than using an approach based upon comprehension of the passage, has comprehension been assessed? They suggested that methods which enable pupils to write, or draw, and talk about their own stories formed on the basis of others, allow the teacher an insight into their 'interpretations and understanding' (Fountas and Pinnell 1996, p. 78).

Concept mapping is used to ascertain pupils' understanding of the relationships between different concepts. The teacher, often with pupils, lists several terms which relate to a given area of study. The pupils are then asked to write the terms on a blank piece of paper and connect them with labelled arrows which indicate particular relationships (see Figure 3.6). The pupils' understanding of the relationships between different concepts can then be assessed (Stow 1997; White and Gunstone 1992).

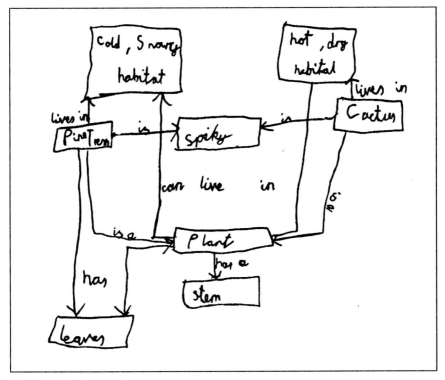

Figure 3.6 Nigel's concept map

With each method the timing of assessment in relation to teaching should always be considered. If assessment is undertaken before teaching the area of study it can provide the teacher with points to build upon. If undertaken at the end of a period of study it can provide evidence of the extent of the pupil's learning.

33

3.6 What are validity and reliability?

The terms validity and reliability are used frequently in assessment. An assessment is valid if it measures what is says it will measure. It is reliable if the assessment provides the same result under different circumstances. Together validity and reliability enable confidence in the outcome of an assessment and both should be considered when an assessment is being developed.

Conner (1999, p. 21) suggested that 'Most teachers are much more concerned with validity; is this assessment a fair reflection of what the children have been taught? Politicians and policy makers tend to be more concerned with reliability; can I have confidence in these results so that I can compare one result with another?' The latter was seen when Chief Inspector of Schools, Chris Woodhead, announced that, in his view, the national tests were unreliable (TES 1998).

Two important aspects of validity are the content, what is being asked, and the construct, how it is being asked. The content of assessment is usually defined by the area of learning with which the pupils have engaged. For example, it would not be a valid assessment of the pupils' learning of the Key Stage 2 curriculum if questions based on the Key Stage 3 curriculum were asked. Assessments cannot cover all of the curriculum so the assessor must decide upon a sample which will be representative of the domain. The construct of a question should enable pupils to demonstrate what is being assessed. For example, it would not be a valid assessment of mathematical understanding if questions were presented in a way which denied access to those with low reading abilities. Nor would the construct of a question be valid if a single word answer was sought in an area where understanding could only be shown through detailed explanation.

Bias can invalidate assessment. Three major sources of bias are gender, social background and ethnicity. All three have been seen to effect national testing. Gender research has suggested that boys respond more favourably than girls to short answer and multiple-choice questions (TES 2000a). Boys also have a preference for different contexts and it was suggested that the increase in boys' English scores in 1999 was due to the use of the context of 'Spiders' in a reading test (TES 1999a). The experiences provided by pupils' social background are also said to affect their scores in context-based questions. Research suggested that the context of a tennis match (TES 2000b) was biased in favour of middle-class pupils. In the 1991 Key Stage 1 Science SAT, 'floating' and 'sinking' caused particular difficulties for pupils with English as an additional language whose first language was Urdu, as the terms could not be translated directly (see section 3.7).

> ### Discussion 3.3
>
> The validity of national assessments is often discussed in the media. In 1997 a mental arithmetic test was piloted at Key Stage 2 (SCAA 1997a). The content was based upon the Key Stage 2 National Curriculum but encompassed mathematics beyond the traditional 'four rules', including estimation of area, millimetre to centimetre conversion, identification of factors and rounding to the nearest ten. The questions were delivered orally using an audio tape. The questions were timed to allow pupils 5, 10 and then 15 seconds to work out and record their answers. Some of the questions were set in familiar contexts, others were context-free. Some required the pupils to remember given information and use it to answer the question, for example 'A shop has a half price sale. A book was nineteen pounds before the sale. How much is it in the sale?', whilst others required a direct response, for example 'Write the number two and a half million in figures'. Some required pupils to answer questions based on given diagrams or numbers. Pupils were not allowed to write anything but the answer on the mark sheet and were penalised if they did so.
>
> Discuss with a colleague why the content and construct validity of the test caused concern amongst the teaching profession. How different are current Key Stage 2 mental mathematics tests to the original test piloted in 1997?

Reliability focuses upon consistency in areas which include question development, test administration, pupil response and marking. Test developers try to ensure internal consistency by checking questions and papers through a number of tried and tested methods (Gipps 1994). Administrative organisations, such as QCA, try to ensure consistency between schools in the administration of national tests by providing instructions on when the papers should be opened and the level of assistance which pupils may be given.

Less straightforward to determine is the area of pupil response and whether it is possible for a pupil to provide the same response to an assessment on different days (Black 1998). The professional experience of teachers suggested that pupils would often vary in their responses, with some demonstrating evidence of learning and others simply recalling or completely forgetting items of knowledge they once appeared to know. This was of serious concern to many teachers on the introduction of statutory assessment when they were asked to provide Teacher Assessments (see section 3.12). How many times would a pupil need to give a correct response before he was deemed to have achieved a particular level?

Marking reliability has two main components, firstly whether different markers will agree with each others marking (inter-rater) and secondly, whether the same marker marks the same work consistently on different occasions (intra-rater) (Gipps 1994). Both can vary according to the nature of the assessment method and subjective influences. High inter-rater reliability is found in tests where a single answer is required, such as a multiple-choice test. But the monotony of marking large numbers of similar pieces can lower intra-rater reliability as human error comes into play. Computers can be used to advantage in these circumstances. Low inter-rater reliability is found where a variety of interpretations can be applied, such as in an observation or within an essay. Subjective influences, including the quality of presentation or knowledge of a pupil, can also lessen inter-rater reliability, whereas the level of intra-rater reliability in such cases depends on the strengths and weaknesses of the marker in question. For example, it is unfortunately not unknown for the last piece of work in a tall pile to gain a poor mark if the marker is tired and the script is illegible.

✎ ACTIVITY 3.3

Harlen (1994, p. 12) suggested that 'validity and reliability can never both be 100 per cent...Assessment in education is inherently inexact and should be treated as such'. Use the format given in Table 3.1, and work with one or two colleagues.

- Decide upon three learning objectives and write them in the boxes on the first line.
- Decide upon the evidence of attainment which would be appropriate for each of these learning objectives and write this in the boxes in line two.
- Brainstorm a list of assessment methods and write this in the boxes in the first column
- Look at each of the three learning objectives in turn and tick the methods of assessment which would enable pupils to demonstrate the evidence of attainment.
- Examine each of the ticked boxes and decide whether the method of assessment is valid in the given situation, mark the boxes accordingly.
- Examine each of the ticked boxes and decide whether the method of assessment is reliable in the given situation, mark the boxes accordingly.
- Discuss your conclusions.

Table 3.1 Analysing assessment methods

	Learning objective 1	Learning objective 2	Learning objective 3
	Evidence of attainment 1	Evidence of attainment 2	Evidence of attainment 3
Assessment method 1			
Assessment method 2			
Assessment method 3			
Assessment method 4			
Assessment method 5			
Assessment method 6			

3.7 How does assessment support inclusion?

As stated earlier, formative assessment provides a key vehicle for learning. But assessment must be accessible and beneficial to all pupils if it is to be effective. The National Curriculum statement on inclusion requires teachers to provide effective learning opportunities for all pupils by:

- Setting suitable learning challenges;
- Responding to pupils' diverse needs;
- Overcoming barriers to learning and assessment for individuals and groups of pupils.

(DfEE/QCA 1999, p. 30)

More able pupils have diverse needs and require their learning to be challenged. The pupils may be 'gifted' in curriculum areas such as science or history, or 'talented' in areas such as art, music or drama. While the abilities of some pupils are evident through the quality of their work in the classroom others may underachieve, as '...their potential is masked by factors such as frustration, low self-esteem, lack of challenge, or low teacher/parent expectations . . . (or) because they have learning disabilities that obscure or eclipse their gifts or talents' (www.nc.uk.net/gt).

Assessment should focus on *what* the pupil learns and *how* the pupil learns (see section 3.3). The teacher needs to be aware that the curriculum and the methods taught are only a part of pupils' learning, particularly in the case of gifted and talented pupils. For this reason the assessments undertaken should be open-ended, promoting creativity and higher-order cognitive skills to provide pupils with reasons and opportunities to express themselves fully and to show themselves at their best.

Discussion 3.4

Stephen, aged 10, read assiduously and wrote long, complex and engaging stories but became frustrated with the rules of spelling and punctuation. He chose to ignore them, as he could understand his writing. Other pupils were unwilling to peer assess Stephen's writing and the teacher found his work difficult to mark against National Curriculum criteria. Is there a problem? What strategies should be used when assessing Stephen's writing?

Gifted and talented pupils benefit from assessment that provides constructive feedback and in which they are actively engaged. It provides pupils with targets for future learning and aids motivation. It helps the teacher to determine the next steps in teaching, in relation to curriculum content and approaches to learning (Koshy 2000; Dean 2001).

Two groups of pupils with diverse needs who have traditionally found barriers to learning and assessment are those with English as an additional language (EAL) and those with Special Educational Needs (SEN).

In assessing pupils with EAL it would be inappropriate simply to translate assessment materials as 'Apart from the arguments of cultural and linguistic bias, there are issues of different syntax, which would render tests unreliable and invalid across varying translations, languages and dialects' (Hall 2001, p. 13). Specialist language support teachers and bilingual assistants can help to assess pupils' learning through their first language. This is particularly useful in providing early identification of specific needs.

Pupils with EAL may be using one or more other languages. Hall (2001, p. 6) gives an example of children from Bangledeshi communities who are 'learning standard Bengali and mosque Arabic, as well as learning English at school and retaining the spoken home language of Sylheti'. Although many pupils with EAL achieve oral fluency within a couple of years it can take up to seven years for English to be developed at a level suitable for cognitive and academic purposes. The teacher needs to recognise how new language is learned and be able to analyse and respond to the pupil's progress (Gardner 2002).

Teachers who understand the progression of their pupils' learning of English as an additional language will be able to support their learning across the curriculum. For example in mathematics lessons a pupil may initially be silent, preferring to listen and watch, offering one-word answers only when new vocabulary has been learned through the use of visual cues and equipment in a clear context. In group work and practical activities he may apply the syntax and structures of familiar languages before developing those of English. Social and practical learning activities provide the teacher, specialist language support teachers and bilingual assistants with an opportunity to assess actions and interactions and so help to determine the needs of the pupil (Gardner 2002). Assessment of a pupil with EAL is necessarily formative and the use of pupil profiles (see Chapter 4, section 4.8) can encourage a more holistic approach to progress.

A national assessment scale was developed to show pupils' progress in English as an additional language in relation to the National Curriculum (QCA 2000). The scale has two initial steps, a threshold and a secure level, breaking down the language demands and providing exemplification and guidance for practitioners as pupils move towards Level 1 in Speaking, Listening, Reading and Writing.

Similarly the P-Scale was developed to help in the assessment of pupils with Special Educational Needs in relation to the National Curriculum. It shows the steps which pupils take as they move towards Level 1 (Berger et al. 2001).

Pupils are defined as having a special educational need if they have 'a learning difficulty which needs special teaching' (DfES 2001). Difficulties may include physical disabilities and those in emotional, social and behavioural areas. Some 20 per cent of pupils have a special educational need at some point of their school lives. As such there is a continuum of needs and responses to needs. The Code of Practice for SEN is pivotal to practice in schools and is, in turn, firmly based upon formative assessment.

> The importance of early identification, assessment and provision for any child who may have special educational needs cannot be over-emphasised. The earlier the action is taken, the more responsive the child is likely to be, and the more readily can intervention be made without undue disruption to the organisation of the school. Assessment should not be regarded as a single event but rather as a continuous process.
>
> (DfES 2001, p. 46)

Formative assessment methods such as observation, questioning and analysis of pupil's work, when coupled with regular monitoring of progress, may quickly indicate a difficulty that can be alleviated through a re-examination of classroom practice or differentiation within teaching. For example, a pupil may need to sit facing the board as he has difficulty reading at an angle. If a higher level of response is needed an Individual Education Plan may be developed. Responses to most pupils with SEN can be made through School Action. When agencies beyond the school are involved School Action Plus is used. For a few pupils it is necessary to gain support through a Statutory Assessment process that could lead to the development of a Statement of SEN.

The Special Educational Needs Co-ordinator (SENCO) monitors the progress of each pupil on the special needs register and provides a first point of contact for teachers who need support and guidance in this area. But it is the teacher's assessment within the classroom that provides evidence of the pupil's learning and potential barriers to learning.

3.8 What is a baseline assessment?

A baseline assessment occurs at the beginning of a phase of education. Its traditional purpose has been threefold, firstly to screen pupils to determine who has special educational needs, secondly to investigate the nature of their learning needs and thirdly to consider how these needs should be supported. Primary schools often ask parents for information about their children through a questionnaire or through interviews and home visits. Teachers also observe and monitor pupils when they enter school. Secondary schools use the data supplied by their 'feeder primaries', collected through transfer documentation (see Chapter 5, section 5.10), and discussions with primary teachers. They may also test pupils in their first term.

Following the 1997 Education Act, a formal system of Baseline Assessment became compulsory for pupils who entered primary school. Teachers were required to assess pupils using a QCA accredited scheme which minimally covered Language and Literacy, Mathematics and Personal and Social Development, areas identified in the Desirable Outcomes (SCAA 1996a). The assessments, which were activities administered orally and recorded by the teacher, had to be completed within the first seven weeks of the pupils' entry into primary school and the results reported to parents (SCAA 1997b). Some 91 different accredited schemes existed around the country (Williams 2002). They were all based upon the National Framework for Baseline Assessment (SCAA 1997c) and they all provided numerical scores.

Lindsay (1998) suggested the purposes of Baseline Assessment fell into two main categories, those with a focus on the child and those with a focus on the school. These categories are demonstrated by the use made of numerical scores, firstly to identify where and what educational support will be necessary and secondly to predict, and later measure, pupils' educational progress by making comparisons with national data (see Chapter 6). Although Baseline Assessment data was used for accountability purposes, Lindsay and Desforges (1998, p. 15) indicated that 'There is no mention of a (Baseline Assessment) scheme needing to provide data on its reliability or validity'. Wedell (1998, p. 64) warned of the potential consequences for accountability procedures by saying, 'inadequate assessment measures would lead to distorted information, which in turn would lead to irrelevant, unfair and possibly harmful decisions'.

The introduction of the Foundation Stage and its associated curriculum led to the end of formalised Baseline Assessment and, in 2003, the emergence of the Foundation Stage Profile. The profile used observation and was to be completed by the end of the Foundation Stage, giving teachers the opportunity to assess pupils in a range of situations and over a period of time against one national assessment scale. While this move was welcomed by teachers as having greater validity, the reliability of such assessment was raised as an area of concern, as 'no two teachers observe alike' (Williams 2002).

Despite the changes that have been made to national requirements, the need for a baseline assessment as pupils begin a phase of education has been recognised as fundamental in 'providing effective learning opportunities for all pupils' (DfEE/QCA 1999, p. 30).

3.9 What are the statutory tests?

Statutory assessment came into being with the 1988 Education Reform Act. In the previous year TGAT was convened to consider the most appropriate forms of testing and how they could be developed. It was a considerable task to determine how such assessment could be successfully achieved for pupils throughout the age range and throughout the country. Some of the advice from TGAT was taken, but certainly not all. Following the introduction of the National Curriculum in 1989, assessments were phased in to allow pupils time to complete the curriculum of the Key Stage. Consequently Key Stage 1 was the first to be tested in 1991, followed by Key Stage 3 and later Key Stage 2, which was the longest Key Stage covering four years.

The first Key Stage 1 assessments were tasks (Standard Assessment Tasks or SATs) not tests and reflected practice in the infant classroom. Teachers were required to set particular activities for the pupils and then to observe and question them at work. Assessment Record Booklets (SEAC 1991), given to all Year 2 teachers, provided evidence of attainment in relation to Statements of Attainment. The booklets also provided an allocation of points to be awarded as attainment was demonstrated by pupils. When totalled, the points awarded indicated levels of attainment in different areas of the subject. Teachers completed paperwork which tracked pupils from one task to the next and they calculated, using given formulae, the final National Curriculum levels attained.

On the whole, the tasks engaged pupils and were considered to provide a valid means of assessment as they were closer to normal practice than formal tests. Similarly, the handbooks sought to improve reliability by giving detailed guidance and were supported by LEA training for those teachers undertaking them. But the tasks were not without their problems. The administration of the tasks in the normal classroom environment led, in many cases, to a lessening of their validity. Pupils who had seen their peers working on the activity earlier in the week declared 'It's going to float – it's been floating for everyone else!' Assessment moderators, who visited schools to see the tasks in progress, witnessed the lessening of reliability through varying practice between schools. When pupil responses were close to the evidence of attainment some teachers kept strictly 'to the book' and others gave pupils 'the benefit of the doubt'. The tasks were also very time consuming and costly. Teachers were required to work with individuals and small groups of pupils to enable close observation and questioning and this frequently meant the rest of the class was taken by another teacher in the school or by a supply teacher, leading to a lack of continuity in staffing and curriculum coverage (Shorrocks-Taylor 1999).

Discussion 3.5

How might the approaches towards assessing a practical task vary between a teacher who has a social constructivist approach and one who has a behaviourist approach? What are the consequences for reliability?

41

The results of evaluations, and political changes (Daugherty 1995) began a move towards more formalised tests for the majority of pupils (National Tests), with tasks for those working below the average level and extension material for the more able, an approach which was reflected in other Key Stages. By the time Key Stage 2 testing was undertaken nationally for the first time in 1995, several changes from the original model had appeared. Key Stage 1 tests focused solely on English and mathematics and Key Stage 2 on English, mathematics and science. The 'process' Attainment Targets of Speaking and Listening, Using and Applying Mathematics and Scientific Investigation, were not assessed through the tests but through Teacher Assessment. Key Stage 1 teachers administered the untimed tests over a given period, marked them, assigned levels and completed Optical Mark Reader sheets (OMRs) which were sent to the LEA, or other designated agency, for collation of results. Key Stage 2 teachers administered the timed tests on a given date according to strict criteria and sent the pupils' work to trained external markers. Schools received from the marker/marking agency the marked scripts, the National Curriculum level awarded to the individual pupil and the collated results. Further changes have been made each year.

3.10 Are the statutory tests valid and reliable?

As discussed earlier, validity occurs at many different levels but two sources which influence the validity of the National Tests are the development of the questions and the tests, and the administration of the tests.

Test development agencies work to build a large number of questions in different areas of the subject and at different levels. The question writers' aim is to produce valid questions which will test the pupils' ability and understanding of the National Curriculum subject while avoiding bias. Questions are trialled with a range of pupils in schools throughout the country. Their answers are analysed to determine whether the questions tested what they were intended to test. The test papers are developed using this knowledge (Shorrocks-Taylor 1999). Mark schemes are devised by drawing upon the range of valid answers given by pupils of different ages and abilities when the questions were trialled.

Schools are required to follow the instructions given in administering the tests to make sure they are not invalidated (e.g. QCA 1999b; 1999c). For example, the tests may not be opened until a given point before administration, the equipment to be used is detailed along with the amount of help which the teacher may give. To alleviate bias special Braille or modified large print scripts are available for those with visual impairment, an amanuensis can be used for pupils with disabilities which impede their ability to write and translations can be made, in mathematics and science, for pupils with English as an additional language.

Increased reliability is an essential feature of the marking of pupil scripts. At Key Stage 1 marking is undertaken in the school. LEAs provide support and guidance in the interpretation of the mark schemes, which are wherever possible written to avoid different interpretations. At Key Stage 2 all markers are required to apply the same interpretation of the mark scheme. To this end the external marking agencies train markers through meetings and a series of marking exercises. The hierarchical structure of markers enables an ambiguous response made by an individual pupil to be discussed and moderated by up to six markers at different levels to determine whether a mark should be awarded (Kingdon 1995). However, difficulties still arise if markers do not realise their interpretation may not be the same as that of others. This occurs most frequently in English writing where affective as well as cognitive issues are considered and is often the subject of media debate (e.g. TES 1995a; 1995b).

Discussion 3.6

End of Key Stage tests in 2003 included 'more questions that require children to use their skills in using and applying mathematics' (QCA 2002, p. 4). What issues are faced when testing 'processes' through 'products'?

3.11 Can the statutory tests be used formatively?

This is one of the few countries in the world where externally marked tests are returned to schools and if they are not used to provide more information about the pupils, the value of the process is lost. Teachers can use the pupils' scripts to learn more about their abilities and approaches in English, mathematics and science. An analysis of the papers can be undertaken at different levels to provide formative feedback on learning and teaching. At an individual level, for example, tracking a pupil's response to mathematics questions which required written explanations, or looking at the jottings on the page which provide an insight into the pupil's thinking, or determining where scientific knowledge is particularly strong, or noticing the stage in the paper at which the pupil began to make significant errors, can all contribute to a better understanding of the pupil's learning. At a broader level, tracking the response to a question of all the pupils in a class or ability group may lead the teacher to consider different approaches to teaching to enhance pupils' understanding in particular areas.

Each year a number of pupils' scripts, in each of the Key Stages, are analysed in detail and the results reported through booklets on standards (e.g. QCA 1999d; 1999e). The booklets include a detailed analysis of the different approaches which pupils used to answer the questions by providing a discussion of their advantages and disadvantages. There is also a statistical analysis which identifies which questions were answered correctly and which were not. Such information can be used formatively by the teacher to enhance her understanding of the methods used by pupils and to develop her own teaching by learning more about misconceptions and errors prevalent in the subject.

3.12 What are the optional tests?

Optional tests are non-statutory tests which can be used in the years when pupils are not undertaking statutory tests. They provide pupils with the experience of a formal testing situation and are very similar in structure and layout to the statutory tests. The optional tests are marked internally and also enable teachers to analyse pupils' work to determine next steps in learning and teaching, and the pupils' progress through National Curriculum levels within the Key Stage.

3.13 What is Teacher Assessment?

Teachers must provide a summary of individual pupils' learning by giving a numerical value in relation to the Attainment Target Level Descriptions in English, mathematics and science at the end of Key Stages 1 and 2. This is called Teacher Assessment (TA).

The development of Teacher Assessment has paralleled that of the National Tests. When TA was first used at Key Stage 1 in 1991, the test result overrode the TA and only one result was reported to parents. This caused much disquiet in the teaching profession as it seemed to imply that the SATs were more valid than the teachers' judgements. When the TA and SAT results were compared teachers seemed to have erred on the side of caution, giving lower levels than those demonstrated by pupils in the SAT. This was not surprising. Infant teachers were new to the notion of national testing and had only worked with the National Curriculum documentation for a short period of time. This was made more evident the following year, in 1992, when there were fewer variations between TA and Standard Test (ST) results. Teachers had learnt from their initial experiences, undertaken more training and were more confident in their judgements of pupils' work in relation to the Statements of Attainment.

However, the distinction between tests and TA became more apparent each year. The tests necessarily sampled the curriculum whereas TA covered all aspects of the curriculum, including the process areas. The tests were administered under formal test conditions using prescribed methods, whereas TA was undertaken within the usual classroom environment. The tests were taken on a given day whereas TA took place at any point and could be repeated to allow for individual circumstances such as illness. Despite this the formal tests were deemed by those reporting on education to be of greater value than the teachers' own assessments.

The Dearing Review of the National Curriculum and its assessment (Dearing 1994) heard the concerns of many teaching professionals on this issue. In his final report Dearing stated that both TA and test results should be reported to parents. He recognised the two as different forms of assessment which could together provide a clearer picture of a pupil's development against the National Curriculum. He also recognised the need for teachers to exercise their professional judgement in determining the TA level. When new National Curriculum documentation was launched in 1995, teachers were instructed to consider which level would 'best fit' a pupil's attainment by using the Level Descriptions of the Attainment Targets. After the prescriptive approach of giving levels according to the criteria detailed in the Statements of Attainment, the 'best fit' approach was quite difficult to grasp. A pupil's attainment could span several levels (see Figure 3.7). How could the teacher decide which was the most appropriate level description? Teachers were being called upon to exercise their professional judgement as never before.

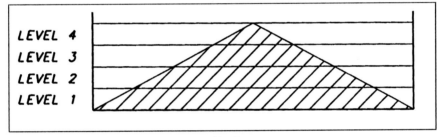

Figure 3.7 A pupil's attainment spanning several levels

✎ ACTIVITY 3.4

- Think of a pupil you have taught recently.
- Consider the approximate level of the pupil's work in one Attainment Target (e.g. Number and Algebra) and read the Level Description (e.g. Level 4).
- Read the Level Description below it (e.g. Level 3).
- Read the Level Description above it (e.g. Level 5).
- Decide which level provides the 'best fit' for the pupil's attainment.
- Justify your decision to a colleague.

3.14 What is moderation?

Moderation is the process by which teachers, when acting as markers, come to agreement on the award of marks or levels. It is a process of negotiation which focuses upon the interpretation of criteria in the context of pupils' work. Moderation enables reliability. It promotes accuracy and consistency through objective analysis.

Moderation developed with National Curriculum assessment, particularly in areas where teachers recognised their judgements could vary from those of others, for example in the process Attainment Targets which necessarily required the use of observation, listening and questioning and in areas such as English writing where a range of interpretations was possible. LEAs, encouraged by the School Examinations and Assessment Council (SEAC) and its publications (SEAC 1993), began to hold 'agreement trials' in the early 1990s to address the moderation issue. A national-to-local model evolved whereby LEA advisory staff met, often with representatives from SEAC, to discuss pupils' work in relation to the Statements of Attainment. They used this understanding to train teachers in the LEA. In some LEAs a new layer of Assessment Support Teachers was formed. These teachers were highly trained by the LEA advisory staff in moderation techniques and were released from their class responsibilities to provide in-service training and support for other schools in the area. Local schools joined together and assigned training days to the cause of moderation. Individual schools held staff meetings to build skills in assessing pupils' work against national criteria and to develop a School Portfolio of Moderated Work (SCAA 1993), which contained evidence of their discussion. Schools were encouraged to look at borderline situations, to decide for example whether a piece of work merited a Level 2 or a Level 3 and to decide why this was the case. The agreement trialling process enabled teachers to be more confident in their TA judgements and helped to provide a degree of consistency through the country when considering written and diagrammatic evidence.

Discussion 3.7

What practical and professional difficulties could arise from a national-to-local model of moderation?

The introduction of Level Descriptions in the 1995 National Curriculum required a more holistic approach to TA and was met with guidance from QCA which provided examples of work within a specific National Curriculum level (e.g. SCAA 1995). The guidance also gave portfolios of work across the subject for two average pupils at the end of Key Stages 1 and 2 and a rationale to explain how the pupils demonstrated their abilities at one level rather than another.

The shift from SoAs to LDs moved the teacher from looking at single pieces of evidence to looking at the pupil's abilities, attitudes and approaches as a whole. The shift changed the nature of moderation as groups of teachers could not examine the whole pupil in a range of contexts. The class teacher always had more knowledge of the situation. Would the teacher be sufficiently objective in making judgements or would the subjectivity, which moderation sought to address, influence TA?

Discussion 3.8

Ask how TA is undertaken in your school. How do teachers make their judgements? Are the judgements moderated? Compare and discuss your findings with a colleague from a different school. Do practices vary? To what extent have schools built upon their experiences of assessment since the early 1990s?

3.15 How can pupils be involved in assessment?

A focus upon ipsative-referenced assessment encourages pupils to be involved with learning and assessment, to become more aware of themselves as learners. As indicated in Chapter 2, section 2.9, the teacher must firstly consider how to share learning objectives with the pupils as without knowing what they are to learn the pupils cannot decide whether they have achieved their goals. Secondly, the teacher must develop this during the lesson through activities and interaction. Thirdly, she must encourage the pupils to discuss what they have learned and how their learning has taken place. Fourthly, she must make provision for developing their learning needs.

The High-Scope programme (Hohmann *et al.* 1979), which originated in America and has been used widely throughout the United Kingdom, builds upon the principle of involving pupils in their learning and assessment. Pupils are brought together at the start of a session to 'plan' what they want to do from a range of given activities and provide reasons for this. They then 'do' the activity. At the end of the session they come together with the adult helpers and teacher to 'review' the activities undertaken, to share experiences and to make decisions about future learning they would like to undertake. The adults can then review the pupils' needs and make alterations to the activities as appropriate.

Discussion 3.9

Does the 'plan–do–review' structure reflect behaviourism, constructivism or social constructivism? Discuss the reasons for your answer.

The cyclical 'plan–do–review' structure of High-Scope is not unlike the recommended lesson structures of the National Literacy and Numeracy Strategy frameworks (DfEE 1998b; 1999a), which indicate the importance of an introduction where learning objectives are shared, the body of the lesson where pupils are engaged in a range of activities and a plenary session where a review of learning takes place. The next lesson should develop from the learning needs of the pupils in relation to the curriculum, not just the needs of the curriculum. The pupils' active engagement in determining the rationale for the work they undertake will necessarily motivate them and provide them with an enhanced experience of the learning process.

✎ Activity 3.5

Look at four National Literacy Strategy and four National Numeracy Strategy objectives which are relevant to your current teaching experience. Consider how these could be shared with pupils. Would you need to alter the phrasing or the level of language? How would you help the pupils to recognise their learning?

Well-defined lesson structures help to develop the reflective nature of 'learning to learn', building upon the checking, revising and self-testing strategies of Nisbet and Shucksmith (1986). These strategies can be developed further within the lesson by encouraging pupils to assess their own work against a checklist, a set of criteria, developed by the class. A checklist for story writing may remind pupils to re-read their work to ensure it makes sense, check and correct grammar, punctuation and spelling and then read it aloud to another pupil to gain feedback from an audience. Checklists may be used in specific contexts but those which cross the divide to encompass general principles help pupils to transfer their learning strategies from one learning situation to another, making links with previous learning and targets and anticipating next steps in the learning process. Examples of effective practice in this area have been documented by Clarke (1998; 2001).

The role of the teacher is crucial to involving the pupils in assessment. The teacher's skill in devising, asking and modelling good questions enhances assessment and learning (see section 3.6). As Fisher (1990, p. 76) emphasised, 'A good question is an invitation to think, or to do. It stimulates because it is open-ended, with possibilities and problems. A good question is productive, it seeks a response. A good question will generate more questions.' A questioning approach is effective for all learners and is particularly advantageous for those who are gifted and talented, for whom a high level of challenge and differentiation must be maintained. Questions which are carefully phrased and posed within a supportive learning environment can help the pupil to assess what he has learned, how he has learned and how he feels about learning, his cognitive, metacognitive and affective responses. They help him to determine where he should go next in his learning and why.

3.16 Case studies in assessment

CASE STUDY 3.1

Robert was a Year One BA QTS trainee on his first block school practice at a large urban junior school. He was assigned to a class of 28 Y4 pupils. His timetable included whole-class teaching and group work. The college tutor observed him working with a group of six pupils on an English task, in an open area outside the classroom.

Robert gave each of the pupils an English comprehension textbook and told them to look at pages 16–17. He read the first two sentences of the text and then asked each of the pupils in turn to read a sentence aloud. The pupils were then instructed to write the date and the title in their exercise books. When they had done so Robert read the first comprehension question aloud and asked for the answer from the text. A pupil volunteered an answer and Robert rephrased the pupil's words to give a full sentence which he told the pupils to write in their books. He repeated this for the remainder of the exercise, making sure that each pupil had contributed an answer and rephrasing each answer to give a full sentence.

In discussion with the tutor after the lesson, Robert was asked to assess the pupils' learning. He told the tutor that the pupils were learning how to complete a comprehension exercise and that all the pupils had successfully achieved the learning objective.

- How valid was this as an assessment exercise?

- Do you agree with Robert's assessment of the pupils' work? Give your reasons.

- Suggest three ways in which Robert could develop his skills in formative assessment.

CASE STUDY 3.2

Lisa was an NQT at a small village primary school of 77 pupils aged 4–11 years. She taught Y2–3, another teacher worked with R–Y1 and the head teacher and a part-time teacher took responsibility for Y4–6. Lisa had been to the LEA training courses for Y2 teachers undertaking National Curriculum Assessments. On these courses Lisa had learned about the statutory requirements for assessment and reporting and how to administer statutory tasks and tests in English and mathematics and Teacher Assessment in the three core subjects. She had also been involved in voluntary after school support meetings for NQTs where, with an LEA advisory teacher, discussion focused upon classroom practice to enable Teacher Assessment.

With a split year class bridging two key stages, Lisa was increasing her skills in coping with differing needs whilst ensuring the class worked regularly as a whole. She used a morning LSA and afternoon parent helper to help maintain the balance of pupils' needs in relation to the curriculum and their individual development. Lisa planned a timetable to enable her to undertake assessment activities with Y2 pupils without detriment to the Y3s.

Her main concern was the reading task which included a running record. She had experienced running records at college and at the LEA training session but was concerned that she would not be able to itemise the pupils' approaches and errors at the speed required. The task administration was also of concern. Should she try to hear children read in the classroom where she could overview the rest of the class but risk distraction? Should she work elsewhere to enable her full concentration on the children's reading? Who would oversee the class in her absence? Lisa discussed her concerns with the head teacher and a compromise was found. Lisa used assembly time to hear individual readers and she audio taped each session.

- How would the validity and reliability of the running record be effected if Lisa heard pupils read while managing the rest of the class?

- Would it be appropriate for Lisa to ask an LSA or parent helper to (a) undertake the running record or (b) manage the class while she undertakes the running record?

- With a colleague, discuss and list different class management strategies which could be employed to enable the teacher to assess an individual or small group of pupils without interruption.

CHAPTER 4

Recording

Record-keeping, the essential interface between assessment and reporting...

(Daugherty 1995)

4.1 Why record?

Galton *et al.* (1999) demonstrated the changing nature of teacher–pupil and pupil–pupil interaction over 20 years, moving from mainly individual to increased whole-class work. The study, based upon systematic observation of pupils and teachers in the same primary schools in 1976 and 1996, documented the frequency and the complexity of interaction. It showed that while many interactions focused upon organisation and routine, others highlighted the learning and the learning needs of pupils. The move towards whole-class work makes different demands upon the teacher in building profiles of individual pupil's learning needs. The teacher cannot, and does not, need to remember all interactions with all the pupils in the class, but she does need to determine which interactions are significant for which pupils, and to remember these in order to analyse and build upon them formatively.

Recording is a mechanism which assists the teacher in remembering significant events and interactions. But it is the analysis of records kept which enables the teacher to track the progress of individuals and groups to make formative decisions, such as moving to a new unit of work, or to build effective summative statements, to provide information upon transfer to a new class or school or within reports to parents.

Three phases are apparent in the development of record keeping in recent years: pre-National Curriculum, 1989–1994 and post-Dearing. Daugherty (1995, p. 96), reflecting upon records kept by teachers before the National Curriculum, stated that practice was 'notably diverse and variable...a matter for decision by the individual teacher, sometimes within a loose framework set by the school'. This was not surprising at a time when schools determined what, how and when to teach, assess and report. The lack of statutory accountability enabled schools and teachers to make professional decisions in all these areas and practice varied accordingly from thorough to ineffectual use. Gipps (1990, p. 6), for example, commented that 'many teachers regard records as rather a chore to complete and make little use of those passed on by other teachers'.

National Curriculum and its assessment, and the almost parallel legislation which increased accountability towards parents and the community at large (see Chapter 6), was substantial in altering teachers' approaches and practices in record keeping. Teachers, guided by their interpretation of SEAC documentation (SEAC 1990a), began to record their assessments of every pupil against every Statement of Attainment of the Key Stage in each of the National Curriculum subjects. This huge undertaking, alongside a need to ensure records were 'simple

---

- Knows name
- Knows birthday
- Knows address
- Tells a simple story using pictures
- Tells a simple story without using pictures
- Writes name
- Listens to stories and poems
- Responds to stories and poems
- Knows numbers 1–5
- Knows numbers 1–10

Figure 4.1 Skills list

to complete' (SEAC 1990a, p. 60), led to an approach dominated by tick sheets which reflected low level, behavioural assessment. The quantity of record keeping which teachers had perceived as necessary soon impinged upon their normal classroom practice. The completion of records, even with a tick or cross, demanded time in and beyond the teaching day. Schools developed records which detailed learning in small steps and often focused upon skills (see Figure 4.1). Assessment of each pupil against each item was time consuming for the teacher yet the completed lists provided little formative information and the creation of such a wealth of information also led to unmanageable data analysis. The purpose of record keeping became no more than the provision of evidence to support judgements and 'a major source of anxiety amongst teachers' (Daugherty 1995, p. 98). It was not unusual to find teachers undertaking record keeping as a paper exercise and elsewhere maintaining notes which they felt were relevant to the formative teaching and learning process. By 1992 what became known as the report of the 'Three Wise Men' (Alexander *et al.* 1992, p. 34) recognised the problems which had emerged by stating, 'Assessment and record keeping are not synonymous, though they are frequently treated as such...' and warning that 'record keeping may in itself become a means to an end...of little value to either teacher or pupil'.

Unrest within the teaching profession, dominated by the huge workload of the National Curriculum and its assessment, culminated in the 'Dearing Review'. When Dearing's final report (Dearing 1994, p. 25) recommended 'The statutory content of the programmes of study...be slimmed, the number of attainment targets and statements of attainment reduced, and the need for detailed record-keeping cut back', the government responded by 'relieving teachers of unnecessary time-consuming record-keeping and form filling' (DfE 1994a, p. 2). The responsibility for teacher assessment, and its associated record keeping, was put back into the hands of teachers but this time within the framework and constraints of the National Curriculum and its assessment. Schools have since been reminded annually that they

> are required to keep records on every child, including information on academic achievements, other skills and abilities and progress made in school. They must update these records at least once a year. There are no requirements about how, or in what form, records should be kept, and there are no statutory requirements concerning record-keeping and the retention of evidence. Decisions about how to mark work and record progress are professional matters for schools to consider in the context of the needs of their children. In retaining evidence and keeping records, schools should be guided by what is both manageable and useful in planning future work. OFSTED inspectors will not require more detailed records.
>
> (QCA 1999c, p. 8)

The Dearing Review appeared to recognise both the purpose of records, to enable formative decisions and to make summative statements, and the need for manageability to enhance the quality of assessment practice.

4.2 What should be recorded?

Once the purpose of record keeping is recognised the decision of what to record becomes clearer. Recording should focus upon pupils' learning in relation to the curriculum, both what they learn and how they learn, and indicate pupils' progress in more general, social and behavioural areas. In some cases it may be related directly to an individual, or group, education plan.

In order to make a formative assessment of pupils' learning the teacher needs to monitor and where necessary assess learning outcomes against learning objectives. Monitoring provides the teacher with a broad overview of the learning taking place in the classroom, whereas assessment is a process which enables the teacher to gain a more detailed understanding of the pupils' learning and learning needs. What to record is determined by what is being monitored or assessed. If, for example, the teacher has administered standardised tests in reading and arithmetic, her recording will comprise numerical scores which give an overview of the pupil's progress in relation to the norm. When a more detailed assessment of an individual pupil is deemed necessary, the teacher may write notes which indicate the level of the pupil's interaction with the task and with his peers along with specific comments which demonstrate knowledge or a lack of understanding. The teacher may also wish to keep a copy of the pupil's work to remind her of the circumstances of the assessment. Records and items of pupil work should always be dated and, where necessary, annotated with information which contextualises the assessment such as whether the work was undertaken independently or with assistance.

4.3 How should records be structured?

Swaffield (1999, p. 93) suggested that 'teachers under pressure tend to want the "how" not the "why"', but when deciding how to record it is essential that the purpose of the assessment it documents is understood, as this will determine the quality and quantity of data to be gathered and how this is best recorded. Will the assessment, and record, focus upon one, two or three learning objectives? Will the assessment, and record, focus upon all the pupils, a few or just one? Will the assessment, and record, simply indicate whether pupils can or cannot demonstrate specific knowledge or a particular skill, provide a single grade or numerical score, or indicate the degree of the pupil's success through the use of simple coding? Will the assessment require, and record include, documentary evidence of pupils' comments and actions? Will the analysis of the assessment, and record, focus on one pupil in one learning objective or across several related learning objectives? Will the analysis focus upon the learning of several pupils, of similar or of differing abilities, and make comparisons between them? Recording sheets can be structured to facilitate the recording and analysis of the assessment. An overview of the recording sheets which form a basis for those referred to in this book is given in Table 4.1. The sheets provide for a range of different circumstances. The teacher needs to determine which is the most appropriate for any given assessment situation.

In some circumstances the teacher may decide that a recording sheet is not an appropriate recording mechanism. It may be more appropriate to annotate pupils' work whilst they are working to record responses to intervention questions, so forming an evidence base and a record of the assessment. Such recording should be undertaken with the consent of the pupils.

Table 4.1 Recording sheets

Sheet	Learning objectives	Pupil(s)	Tick/ Cross	Grade/ Score	Coding	Comments or actions	Appendix reference
Subject monitoring	One per lesson	Group or class	Yes		Yes		A
Mark monitoring	As appropriate	Group or class		Yes			B
General assessment	One	Class	Yes		If appropriate	Yes	C
Focused assessment	Up to three	Up to three	If appropriate		If appropriate	Yes	D
Individual pupil record	As appropriate	One	If appropriate	If appropriate	If appropriate	Yes	E

4.4 When should records be completed?

Every lesson taught will have one or more learning objectives. Therefore every lesson taught must also involve monitoring and assessment. But should every lesson require monitoring and assessment to be recorded? The experiences of teachers at the beginning of the National Curriculum suggested that too great an emphasis on recording could be self-defeating. However in an environment where teacher–pupil and pupil–pupil interactions are so numerous and complex, and the ability to remember, sort and classify all relevant interactions is so demanding, the process of recording can provide a focal point for reflecting upon pupils' learning. This is particularly so for 'novice' practitioners. Trainee and newly qualified teachers are often in awe of the expert practitioner who can apparently hold a wealth of information in her head without the need for recording and make an astute and accurate judgement from what appears to be no more than a quick glance at a pupil's work. They are also perplexed by the demands made in training to keep extensive records of pupils' progress which often go far beyond the requirements made of schools, particularly when training through an Employment-Based Route and within the working practices of the school. Glaser (1995, p. 277) discusses the differences between novices and experts and refers to the 'experts' highly integrated structures of knowledge behind many salient features of their performances'. An 'expert' driver, for example, deals holistically and intuitively with the quantity and quality of skills, movements, coordination and decision-making required in driving a vehicle from A to B, while the novice driver needs to be guided through each stage in turn to develop, practise and improve skills and abilities. So too in assessment practice, the 'novice' teacher needs to consider each stage in turn to develop, practise and improve skills in assessment through the advantageous use of record keeping in order to become an 'expert' practitioner. The two examples of focused assessment sheets in Figure 4.2 and 4.3 show stages in the development of practice towards 'expert'. The first was completed by a trainee who was with the pupils for a few weeks, the second by a newly qualified teacher who was with the pupils each day.

Discussion 4.1

Glaser (1995, p. 227) provides six generalisations of experts' practice:

1. Experts' proficiency is very specific.
2. Experts perceive large, meaningful patterns.
3. Experts' problem-solving entails selective search of memory or use of general problem-solving tactics.
4. Experts' knowledge is high procedural and goal-orientated.
5. Experts' knowledge enables them to use self-regulatory processes with great skill.
6. Experts' proficiency can be routinised or adaptive.

Discuss with colleagues how you have seen the 'expert' status of experienced teachers demonstrated through assessment and record keeping practice.

Whether the teacher is a novice or an expert, writing detailed notes or a few pertinent remarks, the most appropriate time to record will be determined by the needs of the monitoring or assessment, the constraints of the working day and by the approach and self-discipline of the individual. What suits one situation will not necessarily suit another but when to record can broadly be put into the three categories of before, during and after the lesson.

Records made before the lesson may represent a collection of data from various sources which will enable the teacher to plan an appropriate learning experience for the pupils. For example, a new teacher will need the results of recent National Curriculum and standardised tests in English and mathematics to gain an overview of the pupils' abilities in these areas. A trainee teacher may use serial school experience days to determine pupils' current abilities in the use of ICT before she plans a scheme of work for block school experience.

Records made during the lesson may range from simply demonstrating whether or not pupils are competent in particular areas to giving details of the comments and actions made by individual pupils in respect of high-level questioning within an activity. In all situations the teacher and any others who assist in the data gathering process, such as LSAs, need a clear awareness of the learning objectives and evidence of attainment in order to decide when recording is appropriate.

Focused Assessment Sheet

Subject: Maths – Number 19/11
Learning Objectives: Missing numbers to 25. Mixed operations
Vertical taking away + addition mixed
operations to 20 Number recognition & subtraction /
matching number + objects.

Adam.	Ryan.
Adam recognised numbers to 12 today. He was able to count beads and match quantity to number. He used one to one correspondence to arrive at his answer.	Ryan was able to recognise numbers to 15 today. His activity included counting beads and matching beads to number. 1-1 correspondence principle used.
Simone.	Grace
Simone remembered how to use the numberline & coped well with subtraction today. Introduced her to mixed operations - to watch for the signs - after a lot of practical activity she completed some of her work correctly.	Mixed operations T+U's. Grace coped well with this. She looked carefully at the signs and answered her sums correctly. Neat presentation.
Thomas	Nico.
Thomas needed support on his presentation- a gentle reminder. He completed the mixed operations. Tens + Units & was pleased with his achievements	Missing numbers to 25 mixed operations- Nico looked carefully at symbols and confidently answered sums.

Figure 4.2 A trainee's focused assessment sheet

Focused Assessment Sheet

Date: 17|2|00   Subject: Eng.   Activity: Creative writing - extending story

Name	LO1 Content	LO2 Presentation	LO3 Comments/ targets
Charlotte C	muddled + repetitive	Much better - still not joining letters	use story planning grid.
Alex	fairly coherent	neat - but story not written as prose	Remind how to set out
Ashley	good ideas - begin to use more adj's	cap. letters in middle of words /sentences	Cap. letter at beg. sentence or name
Jonathan	lacks ideas v. muddled	Poorly formed letters	use pencil grip - poss. sloping board - see Carrie
Emma H	good start - then repetitive	Poorly formed letters o/a	h'g practice sheets
Chelsea		neat	

Figure 4.3 An NQT's focused assessment sheet

Records made after the lesson may be based upon recall of an event in the lesson or be notes upon the practical or written work which has been scrutinised away from the pupils. While pupils' work can often assist the teacher in recalling comments and actions, detail and accuracy may be lost. It is more useful to make such notes *in situ* although in some cases pupils' written work can provide the teacher with an indication of the methods employed, the strengths shown and the difficulties encountered.

4.5 How can recording be made manageable?

As discussed earlier in this chapter, the introduction of statutory requirements in assessment led to an upsurge in record keeping, some of which was of dubious value and much of which was extremely time consuming. Reflecting on her own practice Frost 'realised that the "beast" that had become assessment was actually "record keeping"' (Frost 1999, p. 50). Although the Dearing Review (1994) went some way to taming the beast it did not conclude the issue of manageability. Some teachers and schools found it difficult to abandon the assessment and recording structures in which they had invested so much time and energy, even if the structures were of little value. Others questioned the purpose of record keeping and altered their practices accordingly. This was recognised by OFSTED (1998, p. 5) which stated 'In schools where teacher assessment is unsatisfactory... records of attainment continue to be based on unmanageable tick lists'. OFSTED urged schools to follow practice 'where teacher assessment is used effectively to raise standards...manageable written recording systems are used alongside the sensible retention of evidence'.

In their research McCallum *et al.* (1995, p. 86) developed three vignettes of teacher assessment practice based upon those they had witnessed in the early days of National Curriculum assessment. They invited teachers to tick the model which best summarised their practice. The attitudes and approaches to recording between the three varied in terms of both manageability and purpose.

> Model A: 'I think it's important to gather as much evidence as I can, things like pieces of children's work, worksheets they've done, little notes I have made, anything I have noticed while they are working.
>
> 'I do my recording at the half term or at the end of term when I sit down with all the evidence I have gathered and think about the child's performance. I wouldn't rely on my memory for that, you have to have it backed up by evidence. I can give them a level using the evidence plus what I remember.'

> Model B: 'I'm recording mentally all the time when watching the processes a child is going through. I don't take notes because I think that can interfere with your relationships with children.'

> Model C: 'Beforehand, I try to interpret the SoAs and break them down into a kind of can-do list: descriptions of what children might do or say to show they are meeting the National Curriculum criteria. I may assess the same SoA more than once, to double check and be fair...I'll observe and question the children while they are working and record at the time or soon afterwards on my checklists...I think you need to be quite specific about what a child has attained on the National Curriculum and record this separately from other things like effort, context and background details: they can be recorded elsewhere, say in a child's record of achievement.'

✎ ACTIVITY 4.1

McCallum *et al.* (1995) labelled the three models as 'systematic planners', 'initiatives' and 'evidence gathers'. Re-read the extracts and decide upon the appropriate label for each model. Work with a colleague to discuss and list the strengths and weaknesses of the recording practices displayed within the three models.

What is considered to be 'manageable' for all teachers? If records of assessment are to be manageable they must be succinct, not taking up a disproportionate amount of time, and they must be well structured, so that they can be analysed easily and effectively. It is not advisable, for example, to replicate records by writing the same information in several places as this is a time consuming practice. A cross referencing system can be developed by ensuring that all records are dated and have clear links with lesson plans. The only exception to this is in the case of the Individual Pupil Record where it is necessary to record significant strengths and significant weaknesses which may occur when other recording mechanisms are being used.

If records of assessment are to be of value, either formatively or summatively, they must be objective, based upon fact not speculation, and purposeful, able to be used for the development of teaching or learning.

✎ ACTIVITY 4.2

A key skill in the recording of assessment is the ability to write objective, succinct and purposeful comments. Examine and analyse the comments in Figure 4.4. Are they written succinctly? Are they based upon evidence or speculation? Do they suggest how teaching or learning should be improved?

Date	Subject	Comment
1.10	English	Wrote a lovely story with clear sentences.
2.10	Maths addition	Sound understanding of mental addition within 20 and some subtraction. Will now need to check, x and ÷.
2.10	Geography	Had problems with map, will need more practice.
3.10	English handwriting	I've noticed David doesn't form some of his letters correctly. This could be the reason he is so slow when writing his stories. I will need to go over the 'o' group and check that he starts and finishes in the right place. This should help him to join letters correctly.
6.10	Art	Good sense of colour shown in painting but some mixing problems with powder paint.
7.10	Maths multiplication	Told me his 5, 2,10 and 3 x tables today.
8.10	ICT LOGO	Likes using the computer. Works well with Steven and Sarah.
9.10	English	Muddling 'their' and 'there' in writing. Need to focus him on these and other doubles in normal classwork.

Figure 4.4 Recorded comments

Gipps (1990, p. 15) maintained that 'record keeping is the most passive use of test results' as she noted how little use was made of the collections of standardised scores which had accumulated for many pupils. Similarly, Black and Wiliam (1998, p. 6) saw a disregard for the use of records which had been kept, 'The collection of marks to fill up records is given greater priority than the analysis of pupils' work to discern learning needs; furthermore, some teachers pay no attention to the assessment records of previous teachers of their pupils'. If recording is to be of value to teaching and learning the records kept must be analysed and interpreted to provide formative and summative judgements.

4.6 How can recording be used to provide formative judgements?

Black and Wiliam (1998, p. 5) stated 'For assessments to function formatively, the results have to be used to adjust teaching and learning'. The sheets identified in Table 4.1 provide a range of recording mechanisms which have been used and adapted by trainee and newly qualified teachers for different monitoring and assessment purposes. Recording assessments is only the first part of the process; it is the analysis and interpretation of results which determines the formative adjustments to be made to teaching and learning.

The Subject Monitoring Sheet (Appendix A), which codes pupils against learning objectives across several lessons in the same subject, can be analysed vertically and horizontally. After each lesson an analysis of the vertical results can identify whether the lesson was sufficiently challenging for all pupils, whether consolidation of the learning objective is necessary or whether the lesson was too difficult for the majority of the class. In the example given in Figure 2.1 in Chapter 2, LO4 seems to have had a more successful outcome than LO3, which will need to be reconsidered in future teaching and learning experiences. By analysing the sheet horizontally it is clear that the pupil who has been absent from all the lessons will need special provision on his return to school. For the pupil who found difficulty in several areas a more detailed analysis of his work would be appropriate, whereas the pupil who appears to have had no problems may need to be challenged further.

The Mark Monitoring Sheet (Appendix B), which indicates marks from standardised tests or other items of work, can be also be analysed vertically and horizontally. By looking vertically at the marks for each test or item the teacher can determine the range of marks in the class and how the marks are distributed. For example, have most pupils achieved high marks in the spelling test, or do a number of pupils have reading ages below the standardised average of 100? Once the strengths and weaknesses of the class are recognised the teacher can alter the pace or content of her work programme to enable or develop pupils' learning. A

Mark Monitoring Sheet can be used horizontally if there is consistency between the tests being used. For example, if the same test is used to check reading ages at regular intervals the development of individual pupils can be tracked and targeted accordingly.

> ✎ ACTIVITY 4.3
>
> Table 4.2 shows the reading ages of 10 pupils at two points, along with their chronological ages. Which pupils have shown the greatest and the least improvement? How well are the pupils performing in relation to their chronological ages? How would you use this information to improve teaching and learning?

Table 4.2 Reading ages and chronological ages

Name	RA: July 1998	CA: July 1998	RA: July 1999	CA: July 1999
Joanne	11.03	8 years 9 months	13.03	9 years 9 months
Rebecca	8.06	8 years 7 months	8.09	9 years 7 months
Nicola	9.09	8 years 6 months	11.09	9 years 6 months
Mandy	8.00	8 years 4 months	9.03	9 years 4 months
Michelle	9.06	7 years 11 months	10.03	8 years 11 months
Garry	8.06	8 years 8 months	9.06	9 years 8 months
Duncan	13.00	8 years 8 months	13.09	9 years 8 months
Troy	8.09	8 years 6 months	10.00	9 years 6 months
Iain	10.00	8 years 2 months	13.09	9 years 2 months
David	8.00	7 years 10 months	10.06	8 years 10 months

The General Assessment Sheet (Appendix C) provides an overview of a group or the whole class in relation to one learning objective. It can be used with a code or with written comments and is an appropriate recording mechanism to determine pupils' learning before embarking upon a new topic, to find a suitable starting point from which to engage all the pupils. The range of abilities within the group or class will also become evident through analysis. Along with the monitoring sheets, the General Assessment Sheet may help the teacher to determine the grouping and organisation of pupils within future teaching and learning experiences.

The teacher's analysis of the Focused Assessment Sheet (Appendix D) should concentrate on the quality of the pupils' learning. What learning did the pupil show when he said 'The Iron Man, he's as tall as a castle!' or when he drew a picture of a man with '2m' at his side and the Iron Man with '100m' at his side?

Did he show understanding with or without assistance? If the pupil still appears to be having difficulty in adding numbers mentally, would a more detailed diagnostic assessment determine the source of the pupil's problem? Examples of completed Focused Asessment Sheets are given in Figures 4.2 and 4.3.

The Individual Pupil Record (Appendix E) helps the teacher to track the progress of a pupil across a range of areas within and beyond the curriculum. This is more evident over a period of time such as a month, term or year. The inclusion of a checklist of subjects at the top of the Individual Pupil Record, which are ticked according to each entry, helps the teacher to see at a glance where assessments have been made and decide whether to observe the pupil in new areas or to investigate particular issues.

The Individual Pupil Record enables the teacher to analyse the effects which different parts of the curriculum have upon one another. For example, it may become apparent that a pupil who has difficulty in reading is constrained in mathematics because the written language he encounters is inappropriate. Or it may be that a pupil has no problems throwing and catching a ball in PE lessons but has yet to refine his fine motor skills when using a pencil or paintbrush. The teacher then needs to work with the pupil to determine, and help him to achieve, suitable targets.

The formative use of all recording mechanisms depends upon the ability of the teacher to analyse and interpret the assessments, to note alterations to teaching or learning and then to put these into action (Appendix F). An Action Sheet (Figure 4.5), which details how, when and with whom the formative assessment is put into action, completes one revolution of the formative planning and assessment cycle and enables the next stage of planning to be more appropriately matched to the learning needs of the pupils.

4.7 How can recording be used to provide summative judgements?

Summative judgments are normally required when reporting to parents, when a pupil transfers between schools, classes or teachers or when other professionals, for example an educational psychologist, require information on a pupil for a particular purpose. Reporting to different audiences is discussed in detail in Chapter 5. Records, along with pupils' work, provide the evidence base for summative assessments. Succinct and objective written records can be used to remind the teacher of the progress the pupil has made across the month, term or year and to determine the extent to which targets were met. Similarly careful cross referencing, and additional information such as the context of an assessment, make records easier to read after a period of time has elapsed, whereas subjective and non-contextualised indicators such as 'Good' or '6/10' are of little value.

ACTION SHEET

Date	Action to be taken	With	Date action taken
20/10	Phonic work: Initial sounds, symbol recognition	Ben, Josie Danny	22/10
19/10	Develop emergent writing, concentration	Tom	20/10
19/10	Ensure instructions are followed by keeping on task.	Naseem	20/10
20/10	Reinforce sequencing of pattern: immediate action	Tom	
22/10	Fine motor: pencil grip	Helen, Tom	16/11
22/10	Phonic work: middle vowel	Richard, Jay Patrick	22/10
5/11	Develop emergent writing	Amy, Aston, Joanna	11/11
5/11	Numberline subtraction	Johanna, Josie	11/11
5/11	Reinforcement 3D shapes	Josie, Ben, Danny	10 & 11/11
10/11	Reinforcement 3D shapes	Josie, Ben, Danny	11/11
9/11	Number recognition	Ben, Josie	11/11
9/11	Practical sequencing no's	Ben	
10/11	Cutting practice	Helen, Danny Ben, Aston, Tom	17/11
11/11	Speech mark reinforcement	Emilee, Laura	18/11
16/11	T & V reinforcement	Emilee, Tom	16/11
16/11	Numberline reinforcement	Josie	18/11
17/11	letter formation 'c'	Ben, Danny	17/11
17/11	Further cutting practice	Tom	17/11

Figure 4.5 Action sheet

4.8 How can pupils be involved in recording?

Involving pupils in recording is not a new phenomenon. It helps all pupils to reflect upon their learning in a structured manner and has been advocated in relation to pupils with SEN, EAL and those who are gifted and talented (DfES 2001; QCA 2000; www.nc.uk.net/gt).

The notion of Records of Achievement (RoAs) or profiles in primary schools was developed at the inception of the National Curriculum and its assessment. Pupils, supported by the teacher and others involved in the learning process, developed a cumulative record of their achievement from a range of sources including written work, drawings and photographs. But, it was emphasised, 'A Record of Achievement…consists…of more than just the production of a folder. Children and teachers discuss progress together, and children are often involved in assessing their own progress and in setting their own targets for continuing learning' (SEAC 1990b, p. 5). The RoA focused upon positive achievements in and beyond the National Curriculum, in order to motivate individual pupils and develop their skills in self-assessment. It also provided a vehicle for discussion between pupils, parents and teachers, developing home–school communication. 'A Record of Achievement is primarily formative in purpose, but it can also have a summative role' (SEAC 1990b, p. 8). Although the manageability issue, which led to the Dearing Review, overrode the full implementation of RoAs in primary schools, the principle and value of involving pupils in assessment and recording still remains.

Individual Pupil Portfolios, a reduced version of the RoA, were recommended by SCAA (1993) and focused upon the three core subjects. The pupil and teacher together would select, date and annotate samples of work which they considered to be representative of the pupil's work each term. As new pieces of work were added the earlier pieces were taken out, so the portfolios were not cumulative. At any time of the year the pupil portfolio comprised nine pieces of work, demonstrating the pupil's progress over the period of a year. The Individual Pupil Portfolio, like the RoA, could be used for reporting to parents (see Chapter 5, section 5.11) in addition to enhancing pupils' roles in recording and analysing their work.

Pupils can be involved in recording on a more regular basis through the use of self-assessment sheets. These sheets show, through writing or drawing, pupils' responses to the learning or learning activities in which they have engaged (see Figures 4.6 and 4.7). Where learning has been broken down into behavioural objectives pupils indicate whether or not they have achieved the objective. Where learning cannot be considered in such an itemised manner, pupils may instead be asked for affective or conative responses, which deal with how they felt about the learning and how motivated they were in tackling the learning and why. These more subjective responses will add a further dimension to the teacher's objective assessment of pupils' learning.

NAME: AREA OF WORK:
1. What did you enjoy doing most? Why?
2. What did you least enjoy? Why?
3. Which things were new to you?
4. Which piece of work did you spend the most time on? Why?
5. What did you have most difficulty with? Why?
6. Who helped you with this work? How did they help?
7. Which is your best piece of work? Why do you think this?

Figure 4.6 Pupil self-assessment sheet for written responses

HOW I FEEL

My name is Charlotte

The date is 2nd May

This is how I feel when...

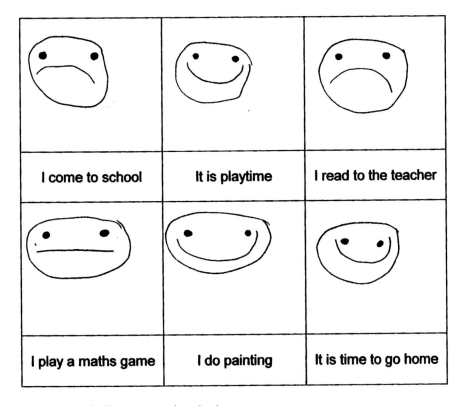

I come to school	It is playtime	I read to the teacher
I play a maths game	I do painting	It is time to go home

Figure 4.7 Pupil self-assessment sheet for drawn responses

Another opportunity for pupils to become involved in recording their progress is through the use of target cards. As the teacher develops an Action Sheet from her assessments, so pupils should be involved in identifying, maintaining and indicating achievement of their personal targets. The targets can be written on the back page of an exercise book, on a reading card or on a separate index card. They may cover curriculum attainment or broader areas such as attitude and approaches or social and behavioural issues. Clarke (1998) suggested keeping individual target setting within the confines of the core subjects with a focus on reading, writing and numeracy. Targets should be achievable and developmental so pupils experience a sense of success and progress in the small steps they take. Clarke (p. 93) wrote positively of her experiences.

> Feedback from teachers suggests that this system is highly manageable and has an immediately positive impact on children's writing and their motivation. Many teachers have reported on quite significant improvement in children's achievement as a result of the target cards, and a keen interest developing from parents, as the child communicates targets at home. Although the teacher sets the first target, children are encouraged to set targets as their awareness of their achievement increases. If children are being encouraged to be self-evaluative and comment on their learning, making suggestions for targets and identifying when they have been achieved will pose no problems.

4.9 Case studies in recording

CASE STUDY 4.1

Angela was a BA QTS trainee on her final six week block practice at a large urban junior school. She was given a class of 33 Y4 pupils and was assigned an LSA for half of each week.

Angela recognised the importance of whole-class interactive work at the beginning and end of English and mathematics lessons and that this constituted a sizable proportion of the available time. She was concerned that she would not be able to assess the learning demonstrated by individuals while engaged with the whole class.

In her lesson plans Angela detailed the questions which she intended to raise in the plenary sessions to determine whether the pupils had achieved the learning objectives. Angela shared her written lesson plans with the LSA, enabling the LSA to recognise the objectives and see how the lesson was to progress. The tasks and responsibilities of the LSA were highlighted on the lesson plan with a coloured marker pen. Specific tasks included noting the responses of individual pupils to questions raised by Angela within the whole-class interactive sessions.

- To what extent was Angela's LSA involved in making assessment judgements?

- How many pupils or learning objectives should an LSA consider during one lesson?

- How could Angela extend her practice to involve pupils in assessment and recording?

CASE STUDY 4.2

Anne was a mature trainee who had previously worked as an LSA. She was in the second year of a BA QTS degree and was undertaking a four week practice at a large urban infant school where a high percentage of children had social and educational difficulties. Anne had a class of 31 Y1 children. She was required by the university to keep assessment records, in core, foundation and general areas, for six children – two of average ability, two above average and two below.

Anne used her preliminary visits to learn as much as possible about the six children. She asked the teacher about previous work undertaken and looked at evidence of this in their workbooks and classroom displays. She noted areas where difficulties had occurred and where children demonstrated success. In lessons she worked with the groups allocated to her by the teacher while taking every opportunity to observe, listen to and question the six children as they worked. Her working notes provided an indication of the range of ability in the class, preferred forms of working and areas for development. After discussing her findings with the mentor, Anne planned her first two days' lessons in relation to the needs of the curriculum and the needs of the children, based upon her initial assessments.

● Which of the recording sheets detailed in Table 4.1 might Anne have used?

● What questions might Anne have asked the teacher?

● Are there any areas which Anne has not considered during her preliminary visits?

CHAPTER 5

Reporting

Assessment must provide an effective communication with parents and other partners in the learning enterprise in a way which helps them to support learning.

(Harlen *et al.* 1992)

5.1 What is reporting?

Reporting is an important part of the assessment process which deals with communicating pupils' learning and learning needs to interested parties. It can be formative, providing information about learning which can be developed through further teaching and learning, or it can be summative, providing information about a pupil's learning at a given point. Reporting can be oral or written, in words or in numbers. Some aspects of reporting are statutory.

5.2 Who are the audiences for reporting?

There are three main audiences for reporting. The first and most frequent is pupils. Reporting to pupils takes place every day, both orally and in writing. In communicating with pupils the teacher reports to them on their progress, their strengths and weaknesses and what should be their next steps in learning. Reporting to pupils is at the heart of the formative assessment process.

The second reporting audience, and that which is legislated for, is parents. Parents need to know how their children are progressing at school. The 1944 Education Act stated that parents were responsible for ensuring the educational provision of their children 'at school or otherwise'. If, as most do, parents choose to send their children to a school they need to be sure that the school is indeed educating them. Schools demonstrate this by keeping parents informed about their children's progress. The legal requirement to report to parents was brought in with the 1988 Education Reform Act. But parents also *want* to know how their children are progressing at school. Home and school together enable children to develop (Nurse and Headington 1999). If parents and teachers understand how children react in different contexts they can together support their development.

The third reporting audience is that of other professionals. This might be the next teacher or school, or it might be a professional who has been asked to investigate or support an individual pupil in some way, perhaps a SENCO or an educational psychologist.

All three audiences have shared needs. They all require from the teacher information which is based upon evidence of assessment rather than personal views and speculation. They all need the teacher to identify from her assessments the pupil's strengths and weaknesses and to determine challenging but appropriate targets.

However there are two main differences between the three audiences. Firstly they do not all share an understanding of the context and the content of teaching and learning which has taken place. Secondly, their understanding and use of the language and numbers inherent in education practice may differ.

Teachers have a full awareness of the context and content of the teaching and learning as they are responsible for planning and organising both aspects. Pupils have necessarily been involved with the classroom context and in the content of the activities but the level of their engagement depends upon the teacher. If the teacher has shared or negotiated learning objectives with them, pupils will have an understanding of why they are doing the activities, what they are learning from them and how to develop their own learning. If the teacher has not shared or negotiated learning objectives, the pupils may have less understanding of their learning. Parents' understanding of the content and context of learning will emanate from a range of sources including the pupil, the school, the 'grapevine' and the media. Of these the school can offer the clearest guidance, supported by the pupil's impression and understanding of the situation. Professional audiences are aware of the content of the teaching and learning taking place although they may not be aware of precise details pertinent to the pupils' learning environment and therefore the context of the learning.

Teachers can communicate with other professionals in the language of education which includes phrases such as 'level descriptions', 'moderation', 'learning objective', 'annotated evidence of attainment' and 'level 3'. Technical terms, or jargon, provide a concise means of communication for those who understand their meaning. Technical terms are not useful when communicating with an audience which does not understand their meaning. Although the teacher may use some technical terms in the classroom when working with pupils, she will invariably provide a context for the terms and an opportunity for further explanation where necessary. When communicating with parents the teacher needs to recognise that parents do not have the same understanding of context and content and that some words used within the world of education may have no meaning, or even a different meaning, when used beyond the world of education. It would be very demoralising for parents to receive written reports which they could not understand because the terms used were unknown to them. Similarly the numbers which refer to pupils' levels in National Curriculum and statements of special educational needs can be very confusing for those who do not encounter them on a regular basis. Successive governments have tried to explain these in leaflets to parents (e.g. DES 1991a; DfEE 1995; DfEE 1999b) and on-line (www.dfes.gov.uk/parents) but the interpretation of these numbers by the media has often carried more weight even though the approach may have been partisan.

Discussion 5.1

Daugherty (1995, pp. 111–13) quoted extracts from several newspaper articles which followed the first Key Stage 1 assessments in 1991. These included:

- The *Sunday Times*: 'one in three can't count'.

- The *Independent*: '28 per cent cannot read or do simple sums'.

- The *Daily Telegraph*: 'over a quarter of the age group cannot identify three letters of the alphabet, let alone read a story'.

- The *Financial Times*: 'They divide 7 year olds into three main groups: those performing at the level to be expected of a 5 or 6 year old (level 1); those performing as expected (level 2); and those at the level of a typical 9 year old (level 3). Overall, performance in science and English was better than in maths. In science, 90 per cent were at level 2 or above, with 23 per cent at level 3; in English, 78 per cent were at level 2 or above and 17 per cent at level 3; in maths 72 per cent were at level 2 or above with 6 per cent at level 3.'

- The *Times Educational Supplement*: 'Nor does the fact that pupils have not achieved level two mean they "cannot read". The standard represented by level two amounts to rather more than that. As many as a third of those recorded as level one may well read with some fluency, but simply fall down on one or two of the more stringent level two requirements – they may, for instance, not be able to use a dictionary."

With a colleague, discuss the possible impact of these extracts upon the parents of your current school.

5.3 What is the purpose of reporting?

The purpose of reporting is both formative and summative.

Reporting progress to pupils assists them in the learning process. It helps them to identify their strengths and weaknesses and to consider how to tackle future learning. The latter is a key feature if the feedback is to be formative. A piece of marked work which is returned to the pupil with ticks and crosses but no indication of the next steps the pupil should take in addressing difficulty or building upon success does not provide formative feedback and can, particularly if the work is of limited quality, serve to demotivate the pupil.

Reporting pupils' progress to parents helps them to gain insight into the teaching and learning process from which most are distanced. It provides them with a greater understanding of the context and content of the pupils' learning and assures them that their children have made progress since the last report. While the formal nature of written reports and oral consultation is largely summative, there is a formative element in the exploration of target setting. Parents want to know how they can support their children in the learning process. This has been demonstrated through the large scale home–school projects such as PACT (Griffiths and Hamilton 1984) and IMPACT (Merttens and Vass 1990), which involved parents and their children engaging in English and mathematics activities in the home environment. Hughes *et al.* (1994, p. 201), who interviewed the parents of some 150 pupils in their study of parental views about education, found 'substantial evidence…that parents have a strong desire for accurate and up-to-date information about how their children are getting on at school. In particular they want to know about their children's strengths and weaknesses so they can provide help where necessary at home.'

Reporting pupils' progress to other professionals enhances the continuity and quality of pupils' learning experience. Reporting to the next teacher, as the pupils progress from one class to the next within a school or from one school to the next, enables the receiving teacher to benefit from the experience of the provider. If a pupil has had particular strengths, weaknesses or targets, be they academic or social, these can be identified through the reporting process so the next teacher or school can make suitable provision. Similarly, if data such as reading ages, standardised scores and National Curriculum results are reported, the next teacher or school will be able to use them to assist in organising pupil grouping and in planning lessons. As with reporting to parents, this is a largely summative process as it takes place at the end of a given period and requires the teacher to summate previous learning. But the process can also be seen as formative as when pupils move to the new teacher or school they should be building upon targets which have been set previously. Reporting at transfer assists in making transitions in school and beyond as smooth as possible. Teachers do not lose time finding out what pupils have covered and how much they know, understand and can do. They can instead plan on a more formative basis, matched to pupils' needs. This in turn helps pupils to adjust to their new situation and gives them more confidence in their new teacher or school.

5.4 What are the statutory requirements for reporting?

The statutory requirements for reporting to parents are given each year (for example QCA 1999b; 1999c). For primary school pupils one written report must be provided each year by the end of the summer term. It must include comments on the pupil's progress in all the subjects studied, the pupil's general progress, the arrangements the school has made to discuss the pupil's progress with parents and the pupil's attendance record if he is of compulsory school age. At the end of a key stage this information expands to include National Curriculum Assessment and Teacher Assessment results, comparative school results and comparative national results (taken from the previous school year). Schools must provide an opportunity to discuss the individual pupil's progress with parents each year.

To fulfil statutory requirements for reporting on pupils' progress as they transfer to a new school, schools must ensure that specific data is provided using the nationally prescribed Common Transfer File (www.teachernet.gov.uk). The data includes unique pupil numbers and the pupil's educational record, which contains reports written to parents and National Curriculum Assessment and Teacher Assessment results. The introduction of Unique Pupil Numbers (UPN) has provided an opportunity for pupils to be tracked as they move within and between schools.

5.5 How can teachers report to pupils?

Reporting to pupils takes place frequently, orally and in writing, informally and more formally. The term 'feedback' is usually used when referring to such reporting. Black and Wiliam (1998) saw feedback as an essential element of the formative assessment process but recognised flaws in classroom practice. In their extensive survey of the research literature they found that primary teachers tended to focus upon presentation rather than the quality of learning, upon giving marks rather than providing useful advice and upon social and managerial functions rather than learning functions. Where practice was most effective feedback to the pupil focused upon the particular qualities of pupils' work, providing advice on what to do to improve, while avoiding comparisons with others and building upon pupil self-assessment.

Teachers regularly give informal feedback to pupils on their progress with a brief remark and a facial expression and through marking work. A more formal process is the pupil–teacher conference, a systematic review of pupils' work which assists the pupil in self-assessment (see section 5.11).

5.6 How can marking provide effective feedback?

Marking is a key skill in the repertoire of a teacher, although it is one which has been criticised by OFSTED (1996a) which stated, 'Marking is usually conscientious but often fails to offer guidance on how work can be improved. In a significant minority of cases, marking reinforces under-achievement and under-expectation by being too generous or unfocused.' In their research of formative assessment practices in the primary classroom, Torrance and Pryor (1998, p. 96) witnessed the mixed messages which teachers can give when marking work (Figure 5.1).

Teacher is sitting in a chair. A queue of three children is waiting to see him. Bella is the first in line. She has given him her handwriting book. Bella has her left hand up to her head and is fiddling with her hair, twisting it round her finger. Her body is arched with her head thrust forward and her buttocks back. She is rocking back on her heels with her toes just off the ground.

Bella	I had to do them lot...
Teacher	...would be fair to say this is probably not your best page in this book (Teacher looks up from book to Bella, nodding as he speaks.)
Bella	mmm (Bella nodding)
Teacher	did you find it a bit tricky today?
Bella	mmm (Bella nodding)
Teacher	why – cos they're quite long words?
Bella	mmm (Bella nodding)
Teacher	OK (Pause for six seconds while teacher writes in Bella's book) I can see you've tried Bella well done good (Bella stops fiddling with her hair.)
Teacher	– so long as you try – all right I'm going to give you a team point for that cos I can see you've tried and you've had to cross out and do it again so it must've been quite hard – yes – well done

---

Figure 5.1 Feedback on handwriting (from Torrance and Pryor 1998)

Discussion 5.2

In the Torrance and Pryor extract in Figure 5.1, what might the learning objective of the lesson have been? What did the teacher focus upon when marking the work? To what extent does this reflect the practice in the schools you have visited?

The traditional view of marking, where ticks and crosses are given with a single comment of 'good' or 'poor', is far from useful in the formative process. Similarly feedback which provides no further guidance for the pupil and ends with the expression 'well tried' focuses upon the effort made by the pupil rather than on the content of the work and the learning objective. Sadler (1989) recognised that, even when pupils were given feedback, they did not necessarily understand how it should be used formatively. The manageability of providing detailed and constructive oral and written feedback for every pupil in a range of subject areas may prove inhibitive for the busy teacher. As with other areas in the classroom practice of assessment, a balance needs to be struck. In doing so the teacher needs to consider why marking is important in providing feedback to pupils on their progress and how it can be effectively managed.

Two strategies for marking are 'hot marking', which is undertaken alongside and with pupils, and 'cold marking' which is undertaken away from them. Both are contextualised and as such should relate to the learning objectives underpinning the work. Both should encourage and motivate by identifying strengths, recognising weaknesses and indicating how further progress can be made. Both are influenced by the time which the teacher has available during the teaching day and by the teacher's relationship with the pupils.

Hot marking allows the teacher to ascertain the pupil's reaction to the comments made and to build upon them. It enables her to use verbal and non-verbal communication which is appropriate for the individual pupil in respect of the individual piece of work which is being marked. It allows the teacher to 'read' the pupil's verbal and non-verbal communication to decide whether the pupil is prepared for the nature of the teacher's feedback before it is given, particularly if the feedback is negative, or whether to convey the feedback in a different, more palatable, way. Walker and Adelman (1976) reported a seemingly bizarre interaction between teacher and pupil where the word 'Strawberries!' was used to describe work as it was hot marked. 'Strawberries!', it transpired, was a humorous class code to convey feedback that the work was good but didn't last long enough.

Hot marking also allows the teacher to work formatively with pupils to provide explanations where necessary, to develop areas of strength and to help pupils evaluate their learning, a key skill for self-assessment and metacognition (see section 5.11). Alexander et al. (1992, p. 33) recognised that 'provided it offers specific diagnostic comments not only encouragement...the act of marking in the pupil's presence is an even more effective approach...Pupils should as far as possible be involved in the assessment of their own work...'. As suggested in Chapter 2, when hot marking is used alongside the 'ripple effect', its benefits can be multiplied.

Cold marking occurs when the teacher marks pupils' classwork or homework away from them. Feedback is usually written and may include a reward such as a star or a grade. Written comments should be in language which is appropriate for the pupil and recognise the needs and personalities of the individual. While they have been considered as motivators, there is evidence to suggest that rewards are detrimental to learning as they encourage pupils to 'look for ways to obtain best marks rather than at the needs of their learning which these marks ought to reflect' (Black and Wiliam 1998, p. 9).

Two steps are necessary for the feedback from cold marking to be effective. Firstly, the teacher needs to focus upon the strengths and weaknesses of the work and provide further guidance to aid pupils' progress in relation to the learning objective. Secondly, pupils need time to reflect and act upon the teacher's comments with her assistance. Both steps require the time and commitment of teachers and pupils. Without these steps cold marking is not part of the formative assessment process but instead becomes a small summative assessment exercise.

Cold marking is enhanced by a shared understanding of the learning objectives and a focus upon improving the quality of the pupils' learning. Pupils should know the expectations of the teacher before embarking upon the work and the teacher should mark their work accordingly. If pupils have been asked to write a lively and exciting story the marking should highlight compositional rather than transcriptional and secretarial features, which could be considered at the next drafting stage. Feedback should centre upon the context which was initially indicated rather than upon extraneous features. This is evident in Figures 5.2 and 5.3 where the teacher commented upon Jack's achievement of the given tasks and alerts him to spelling mistakes made when using reference materials.

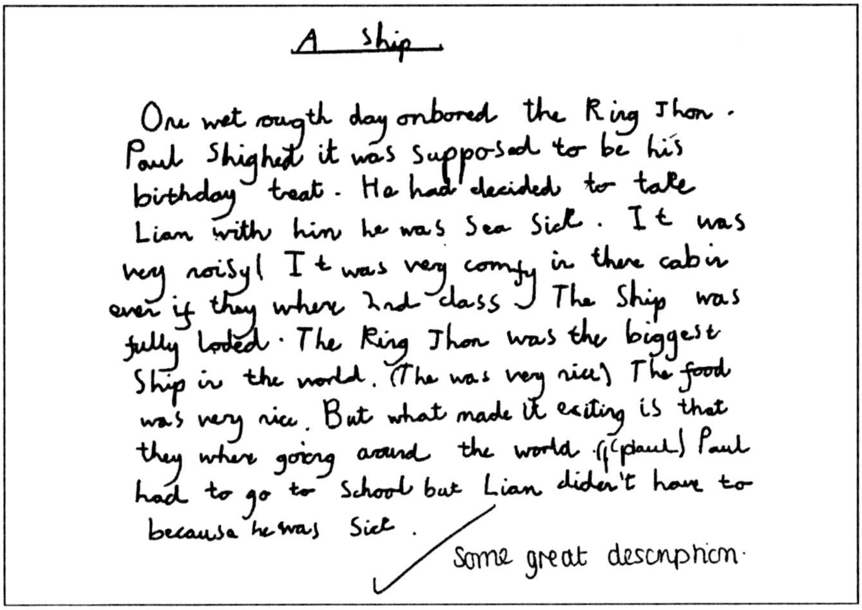
A Ship

One wet rougth day onbored the Ring Jhon. Paul Shighed it was supposed to be his birthday treat. He had decided to take Lian with him he was Sea Sick. It was very noisy! It was very comfy in there cabin even if they where 2nd class. The Ship was fully loded. The Ring Jhon was the biggest Ship in the world. (The was very nice) The food was very nice. But what made it exiting is that they where going around the world. ((paul) Paul had to go to School but Lian didn't have to because he was Sick.

Some great description.

Figure 5.2 Jack's writing focusing on descriptive language

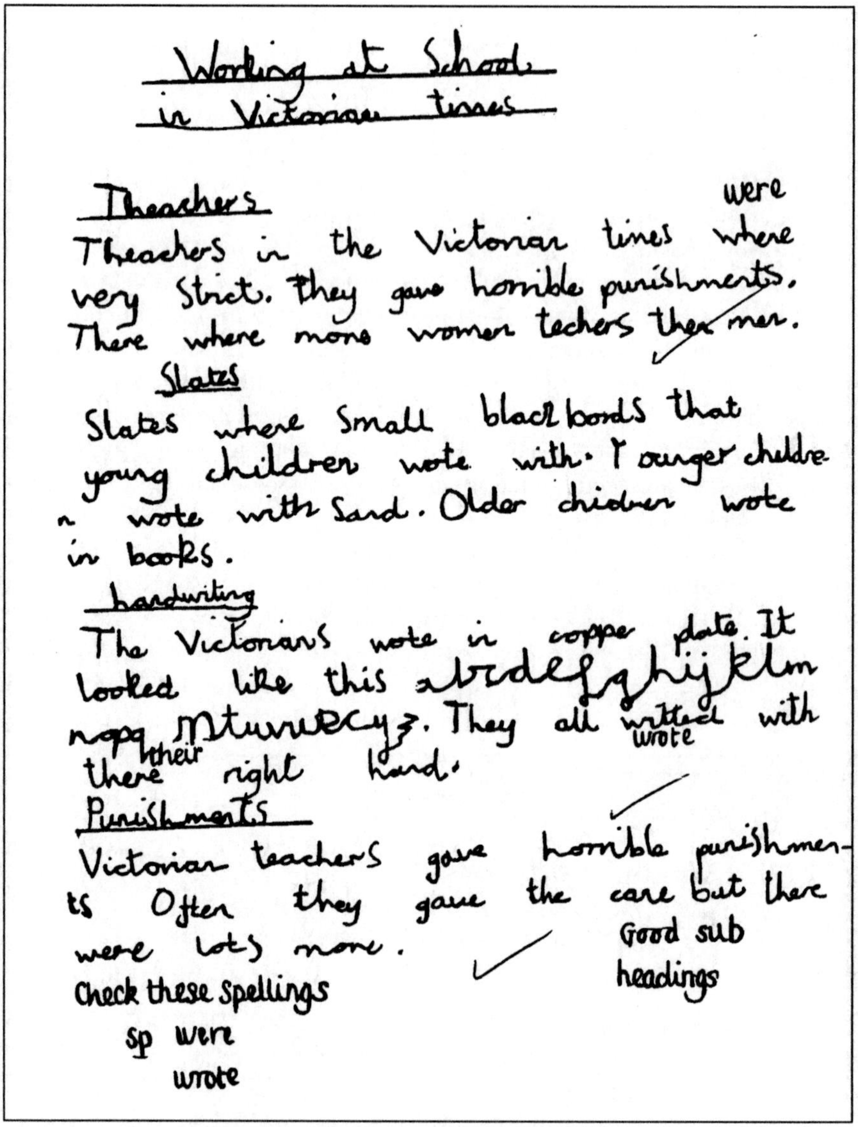

Working at School in Victorian times

Theachers

Theachers in the Victorian times where _were_ very strict. They gave horrible punishments. There where more women techers then men.

Slates

Slates where small blackboards that young children wote with. Younger childrea wote with sand. Older chidren wote in books.

handwriting

The Victorians wote in coppe plate. It looked like this abcdefghijklm nopq rstuvwxyz. They all wrote with there _their_ right hand.

Punishments

Victorian teachers gave horrible punishments Often they gave the cane but there were lots more.

Check these spellings
sp were
wrote

✓ Good sub headings

Figure 5.3 Jack's writing focusing on organising information from books

A term such as 'good', used in isolation, is context free and gives no indication of why or how the work was good. However, if shared meanings are discussed and agreed by pupils and the teacher, suitable codes could be employed to provide feedback which is succinct and purposeful. To complement the 'Strawberries!' mentioned previously is the example of a teacher who drew a woolly sheep to indicate when the pupil was straying from the point. It is the quality, not the quantity, of feedback to pupils which is most important, particularly when cold marking.

Discussion 5.3

Look at the mathematics work in Figures 5.4 and 5.5. Discuss with colleagues how the sets of addition and subtraction algorithms should be marked.

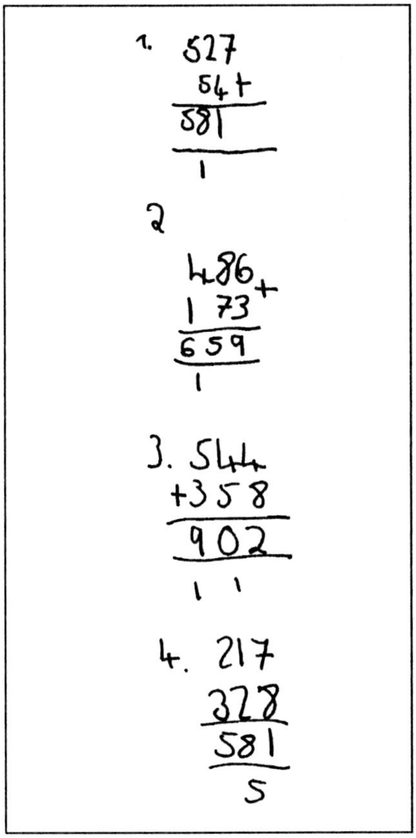

---

1. $527 + 547 = 581$ (1)

2. $486 + 173 = 659$ (1)

3. $544 + 358 = 902$ (1 1)

4. $217 + 322 = 581$ (S)

Figure 5.4 Addition algorithms

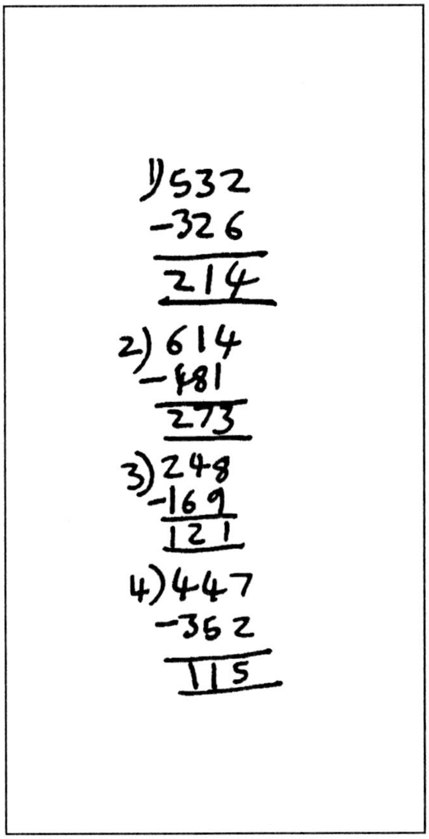

1) $532 - 326 = 214$

2) $614 - 481 = 273$

3) $248 - 169 = 121$

4) $447 - 362 = 115$

Figure 5.5 Subtraction algorithms

Target setting cards (see Chapter 4, section 4.8) can be effectively used in both hot and cold marking situations to enhance the formative nature of the feedback process and to engage pupils in self-assessment.

5.7 How do teachers report to parents?

Home–school contracts (Bastiani 1996) have been a requirement for all schools since 1999 and build upon documents such as *The Parent's Charter* (DES 1991b; DfE 1994b). They have highlighted the roles and responsibilities within 'the triangular relationship of parents, children and teachers' (Nurse and Headington 1999, p. 13). But 'building bridges' between home and school (Jowett and Baginsky 1991) demands more than dictate, it demands a commitment to the beneficial relationship which home–school cooperation can bring for the pupil. The teacher can demonstrate this commitment when reporting to parents in a variety of ways, formally or informally, in writing or orally (see Table 5.1). In this book the two areas which are considered in detail form the basis of the statutory requirements for reporting to parents, written reports and oral consultations.

Table 5.1 Reporting to parents

	Formal	Informal
Written	• Written report to parents, at least once a year • After 15 days if requested by parent	• Homework books and reading cards • Requests for help and resources • Responding to notes from parents • Displays
Oral	• Parent–teacher consultation, opportunity given at least once a year • Following formal requests from parent or teacher regarding specific learning or behavioural issues	• At beginning/end of school day, sometimes during school day • Open days/evenings and assemblies • Responding to phone messages • Following informal request from parent or teacher regarding specific learning or behavioural issues

5.8 How should reports to parents be written?

The most formal mechanism for reporting to parents is through written reports. The content of written reports is governed by the current *Assessment and Reporting Arrangements* (see, for example, QCA 1999b). The timing of reports within the school year and their structure have been left to individual schools, even though an attempt to introduce a nationally standardised report was made in 1991 (Daugherty 1995).

In writing a report of quality it is essential that the teacher bases her comments upon evidence, not speculation. Comments should have a reference point. Criterion-referencing enables the teacher to comment on the pupil's progress against given criteria such as the National Curriculum. Ipsative-referencing enables the teacher to comment on the pupil's progress in relation to his previous work and targets. Norm-referencing enables the teacher to comment on the pupil's progress in relation to others of the same age. It is not appropriate to make direct comparisons with other individuals in the class, but the teacher can draw upon general information about pupils of the same age from school and national statistics.

Three key features must prevail when writing reports. Firstly, the child should be recognisable. Pupils are individuals and parents need to be confident that their child is recognised as such by the teacher. General comments which could apply to any pupil may suggest to parents that the teacher has little knowledge of the individual. Monitoring, assessment and their associated record keeping practices should alleviate 'invisible children' (Pye 1988) and ensure the teacher has information about the learning development of all her pupils. Secondly, written comments should be clear and straightforward. As previously discussed, the use of technical terms is less than helpful when communicating with the world outside education. Comments should also demonstrate respect for parents and should not patronise them. The level at which to pitch written comments is easier to determine when the teacher has met and talked to parents. As this is not always possible a useful source from which to determine appropriate pitch is the plethora of literature for parents, produced by the DfEE and DfES, which has been awarded for its clarity by the Plain English Campaign (for example, *It all adds up*, DfEE 1999c). Schools should, where possible, also provide a copy of the report in the parents' home language. Thirdly, the report should motivate and encourage both the parents and the pupil by recognising and building upon strengths and by suggesting ways to overcome weaknesses. Comments should focus objectively upon learning issues, such as attainment, behaviour, attitudes and approaches, which can be developed, rather than referring subjectively to personal qualities which are unlikely to change. Reference to the context of learning helps to retain a focus upon the pupil's learning, but 'The report should concentrate on what the child has or has not learnt, rather than what has been taught' (QCA 1999c, p. 60). Targets which are set should be realistic and achievable. They should develop the individual pupil and support the home–school partnership. Parents, pupils and teachers should be able to look at the reports as they accumulate year by year to see the progress the pupil has made and recognise the roles that each has played in moving the pupil forward.

✎ ACTIVITY 5.1

Put the following comments into the three categories of general, technical and personal:

- he is making steady progress
- her language acquisition is weak
- he must try harder
- she is a sensible little girl
- he has poor coordination and motor skills
- she has successfully moved from the concrete to the abstract
- he is lazy
- she is a capable and intelligent pupil
- he is enthusiastic
- her work is of a satisfactory standard

Decide whether and how each statement could be amended to provide parents with comments which are specific to the individual pupil, written in appropriate language and clearly based upon referenced evidence. In each case indicate how the pupil could improve his or her work. Complete this activity by reading and critiquing the sample texts of school reports given in the Assessment and Reporting Arrangements (e.g. QCA 1998a; 1998b; 1999b; 1999c).

Reports are usually handwritten or word-processed but computer generated reports to parents are used in some schools. These enable the teacher to choose statements from a comment bank. There are advantages and disadvantages to this system. The main advantage is the clarity of the report and, for the teacher, any spelling or grammatical errors are quickly resolved without the need to rewrite the whole report. Computer generated reports may contain more information, some for example include paragraphs which describe the content of the curriculum with individual comments written in relation to them. The main disadvantage to parents is the impersonal nature of the report. Computer generated reports are initially quite time consuming to 'write', particularly for new users who may need the help of other teachers and support staff. However, parents, when reading the product, may consider that the teacher has spent less time thinking about the individual pupil. Finally, unless the program allows for adjustments, the same range of comments must be used for all parents.

5.9 How do teachers conduct oral consultations with parents?

Formal oral consultations with parents, where the teacher and parents discuss the progress of an individual pupil, can be a daunting prospect for student and newly qualified teachers, but they may be surprised to learn that 'Many parents [are] "afraid" to speak to teachers' (TES 1999b). The DfES has responded by creating a website to provide information and answer parents' questions (www.dfes.gov.uk/parents). Bastiani (1989, p. 75) identified differing viewpoints of teachers and parents to the formal oral consultation process and concluded that 'greater progress could be made if the reasons for such meetings were clear and agreed by both teachers and parents...It is...a major opportunity in the home–school programme to focus upon the efforts and achievements of individual pupils.' He recommended giving both parents and teachers the opportunity, in advance of the meeting, to raise areas which they would like discuss and so to form a 'two-way agenda'.

The agenda set by the statutory requirements is that there must be an opportunity 'for parents to discuss the [written] report with a teacher at the school' (QCA 1999c). But the timing, duration and structure of the meeting is left at the discretion of the school. Consequently a wide variation of practice has emerged, from schools which have consultations at different points through the year, where the written report acts as a confirmation of points covered, to schools which provide the written report at the consultation late in the summer term. Varying practice puts different emphases upon the consultation process: the latter model is generally summative whereas the former model is more formative, providing an opportunity for parents and teachers to review and develop targets through the year. The time available for consultation may vary between schools from a strictly monitored five minutes to the time which the teacher has available before the next parents arrive. The focus for discussion may be, as suggested by QCA, the written report, or the pupil's work or issues raised by parents and/or teachers before or during the consultation. Some schools also like to involve pupils in the consultation process to support the triangular relationship mentioned previously.

Whichever model a school chooses to use there are a number of fundamental points which need to be considered by those undertaking oral consultations with parents for the first time. The first point is in the adage 'first impressions count'. The room where the consultation is to take place should be tidy and welcoming, with comfortable chairs, suitable for adults, positioned in preparation for the meeting. If parents require special arrangements, such as an interpreter or wheelchair access, this should be arranged in advance through a senior member of staff. The teacher must also be prepared for the consultation. It may be advantageous for her to re-read the written reports, her assessment records and the pupils' work to remind herself of key strengths, weaknesses, targets and questions she would like to ask of the parents. Named index cards can hold these notes discreetly and enable the teacher to write quickly any points which come from the discussion.

Secondly, a smile, a handshake and a personal introduction, 'Hello, I'm Lisa Smith, Jason's teacher', will help the parents to feel at ease. The teacher should start with a positive statement about the pupil's attitude, approach, behaviour, attainment or achievements. The opening remark, 'I'm very pleased with the way Jason is settling into the class, particularly as he started at the school several weeks into the term. He seems to be making friends quickly', reassures parents that the teacher knows their child as an individual and that she recognises one of his strengths.

Thirdly, rather than launching into a tirade of the pupil's strengths and weaknesses, the teacher needs to remember that the consultation process is two-way. Some parents will need to be invited to participate, others will offer comments and observations more comfortably. The teacher should allow parents time to reflect upon comments and to look at their child's work. The pupil is also the parents' child. Through the year he will spend more time beyond school than in it and, as learning takes place in many different situations, the teacher will gain a greater understanding of the whole child by learning more about the pupil beyond school. His attitude to school, his home situation, and the support or setbacks he has encountered, all impact on his learning. The teacher needs to be an active listener, not just a reporter of academic progress.

Fourthly, the teacher needs to provide facts about the pupil and his work which can be supported by evidence. In addition to index cards with key points, it is useful for the teacher to have her record keeping file at hand and to have the pupil's work available for quick reference. Post-its could be used to highlight particular items for discussion within exercise books. If Records of Achievement or Individual Pupil Portfolios (see Chapter 4, section 4.8) are not available, pupils may like to use post-its to indicate to their parents the work in which they took most pride. When the consultation is taking place in the classroom, the pupil's displayed work could be shown to parents. It is important to recognise that although parents should only be given the opportunity to look at the work of their own child, any displayed work provides parents with reference points for comparing their child's work with others. The End of Key Stage teacher should also be prepared to explain National Curriculum levels and comparative school and national data to parents. Although this may be undertaken separately with a larger group of parents by the head teacher, assessment coordinator or LEA representative, individual parents may still want to ask questions about their own child's results.

Fifthly, the teacher needs to be prepared for difficulties and have prepared ways of handling these with the head teacher and other senior members of staff. If the teacher finds a question difficult to answer, such as the explanation of comparative national results, she may refer the parents to another more experienced or specialist teacher. If parents want more time for discussion the teacher should indicate that, for example, only 10 minutes is available this evening but that she would be pleased to arrange another appointment. If, as happens very rarely, parents start to become aggressive or demand additional time there and then, the teacher should avoid confrontation and calmly accompany and introduce the parents to the head teacher. It is advisable under these circumstances for the teacher to take a few minutes to recompose herself before going back to her classroom to meet the next parents.

Targets and ideas for parents to help their children in the learning process form the final point to consider. Ideally target setting should be conducted between the pupil, parent and teacher. In reality most target setting takes place between the teacher and pupil, teacher and parent, and parent and pupil. The parent–teacher consultation provides an opportunity for the teacher to explain why she has agreed certain targets with the pupil, to recommend, negotiate or confirm targets made with the parents, and to ascertain or suggest targets which can be made between the parents and pupil. Targets should be supported by suggestions of activities in which pupils, and parents, can engage. For example, recommending that parents could help the pupil to learn a multiplication table may lead to the pupil reciting 'Once two is two, two two's are four, three two's are six, four two's are eight...' without understanding how sets are combined. Indicating to parents how sets of two can be explored, counted and multiplied in the home will encourage them to provide a more enriched experience. Demonstrating to parents how the pupils are taught to form letters using cursive hand in the house style takes no more than a few minutes and is more effective than giving them a sheet of completed letters. The teacher should take the opportunity of an oral consultation with parents to consolidate home–school curriculum initiatives and to help parents to understand more about current classroom practice. Shops bombard parents with books which provide practice for End of Key Stage tests. If such practice is not appropriate for the pupil the teacher needs to indicate this and suggest activities which will be beneficial for his learning.

✎ ACTIVITY 5.2

Working with colleagues who are teaching a similar age group, list ten ideas for parents to develop their children's English and ten ideas for developing their children's mathematics in the home environment. Consider when and how these could be explained to parents during an oral consultation.

5.10 How do teachers report to other professionals?

Reports to other professionals are to internal or external audiences. Most teachers report to another professional at least once a year as the pupils move to a new class teacher within the school, the internal professional audience. Reports to external professional audiences centre on transfer to a new school. When an individual pupil needs additional support a report may be requested internally or externally.

The size of the school and the mobility of the teachers will help to determine how the process of reporting to an internal professional audience is undertaken, from an informal discussion to the completion of a transfer file. For example, in a small school with a static workforce teachers may already be aware of the characteristics of individual pupils and find an informal discussion is appropriate, whereas in a large school with a transient teacher population, teachers may find a structured approach to the transfer of information from one teacher to the next is more suitable.

The receiving teacher needs specific information about the curriculum, the class, and individual pupils. Although the National Curriculum and the Literacy and Numeracy Strategies have detailed the curriculum content expected of each year group, the receiving teacher needs to know the extent of coverage which has occurred in the previous class so she can build upon it. Significant information about the class as a whole needs to be passed on to the next teacher. National Curriculum levels and the results of standardised tests assist the receiving teacher in devising an appropriate learning programme. Information about social and behavioural areas will assist her in managing pupil relationships from the outset. Significant details of individual pupils are essential if the formative nature of learning is to be met. The strengths and weaknesses of individual pupils' learning should be identified, including details of SEN statements and IEPs, EAL support and provision, areas of gift and talent and pupils' preferred learning styles. Targets which have been set in the previous class need to be given to the receiving teacher to enable a smooth transition. Records of Achievement and Individual Pupil Portfolios provide a very personal account of individual pupils. Other areas of impact upon the pupil's learning such as personal and health information are equally vital.

Reports to internal professional audiences are often requested of trainee teachers at the end of a block practice to enable the teacher to build upon their work. Writing these reports helps trainees to develop and practise their reporting skills and to recognise how pupils develop, even over a relatively short period of time. This is clearly demonstrated in Figure 5.6, in which a Year One BA(QTS) trainee reported on one of the six pupils she profiled over a four week block practice.

Charlotte Smith

Year R: SEN Level 2

Charlotte's speech is immature. She sometimes stutters and her vocabulary is limited when compared to children of the same age. She will often answer a question with 'don't know' before she really thinks about an answer. Her attention span is quite short. She can recognise her name but cannot write 'Charlotte' with correctly formed letters. She can count to 10 but lacks accuracy when counting out and needs to practise identifying which of two sets of objects has more.

Charlotte is friendly and kind to others. She likes to play in the activity area, especially dolls and dressing up. Charlotte has three special needs targets, working one-to-one with the classroom assistant and sometimes in a group.

1. To be able to write 'Charlotte' correctly.

2. To recognise the sounds s, a, t, p, i, n.

3. To broaden her vocabulary.

Figure 5.6 A trainee's report to a teacher

✎ ACTIVITY 5.3

Write a report which will transfer the information about one pupil to another teacher. Give it to a colleague and together discuss whether

● the content is (i) relevant (ii) sufficient

● the comments are (i) objective (ii) succinct

A report to an external professional audience occurs when a pupil transfers to a new school. The recipient, and often the school, may or may not be known to the teacher who is sending the information. Transfer occurs at two points. Firstly, the pupil may move school within a Key Stage, due to a family move for example. Secondly, the pupil may be moving from a school which caters for one age group to one which caters for the next age group. The latter is often, though not always, related to a change of Key Stage.

The formal move from one school to another necessitates the transfer of details contained in the pupil's individual educational records. Statutory requirements must be adhered to with the inclusion of written reports to parents and details of any National Curriculum Assessment and Teacher Assessment results undertaken at the school using the Common Transfer File.

Prescribed transfer documents are a recent phenomenon, emanating from the *Assessment and Reporting Arrangements 2000* (QCA 1999b; 1999c). The information required to complete the forms is summative and deals mainly with National Curriculum Assessment and Teacher Assessment levels, areas of support, ethnicity and attendance. Additional information can be enclosed if it is deemed necessary.

Before sending transfer information to a new school it is important to consider how it will be used by the next teacher or group of teachers. Where pupils move frequently between primary schools during the school year and within the Key Stage, for example those whose parents are serving members of the British Forces, the summative data which is transferred helps the receiving school to quickly and effectively place individual pupils within the appropriate class and class groups. Day to day information, such as books read and schemes used, may help the receiving teacher to determine the level of work which is appropriate and enable the pupil to settle quickly and comfortably. At this point the receiving teacher can administer further assessments to refine the learning needs of the pupil still further in relation to those outlined in the pupil's education record.

Where a pupil or a number of pupils transfer to a school which caters for the next age group or Key Stage, the situation may vary, particularly if the school is receiving pupils from a number of different feeder schools. For example a primary school may be one of 20 or more schools sending Year 6 pupils to a secondary school which has pastoral groups and subject teaching. The records which are sent by one teacher may be pertinent to a dozen or more receiving teachers who need to group the pupils and those from many other primary schools.

✎ ACTIVITY 5.4

Imagine you are a Year 6 teacher. You have spent a year working with a class of 30 pupils, giving detailed feedback and helping them to build portfolios of work. You have written reports and, through the year, have engaged in oral consultations with parents. List the information about the individuals in your class you would like to provide for the next teacher in their new schools. Remember to include the statutory information which is required at transfer.

Drawbacks to the transfer process were noted by McCallum (1996) in her study of the transfer and use of assessment information between primary and secondary schools. She found that secondary schools wanted standardised information from primary schools early in the summer term to organise tutor groups and that much information provide by primary schools was not used. McCallum noted the difficulties which can ensue.

> There appears to be little acceptance of other teachers' assessments on the whole, and this often leads to resentment from primary schools and to the clean-slate, fresh start approach at secondary level or to the giving of tests on transfer.
> Primary schools send up a great deal of information on children and for them this is important – it symbolises a child's whole career at school. However, formats are all different and a lot of information is not easily deciphered and consequently not easily used by secondary schools (1996, p. 14).

Discussion 5.5

In the light of McCallum's findings review the list of information for transfer compiled in Activity 5.4. How beneficial would it be for the receiving school? Discuss the steps which could be taken to build relationships between primary and secondary schools to facilitate pupil transfer?

To promote consistency between Key Stages at transfer two areas need to be considered, firstly the transfer of records and secondly the professional links between schools (SCAA 1996b). Case studies of good practice in the use of Key Stage 2 assessments at transfer were given in SCAA (1997d). Further to these suggestions a range of innovative practices have developed to help pupils and teachers in the transfer process. Schools hold meetings between teachers working in the two age groups where the transfer takes place at different times of the year to prepare for and to follow through the transfer process. Some schools arrange for teachers and classes to visit each other's establishments when in session and others even arrange for teachers to teach in each other's schools.

To gain additional support for an individual pupil the teacher may be required to write a report to an internal (e.g. SENCO) or external (e.g. Educational Psychologist) professional audience. The nature of the report will be determined by the needs of the pupil and by local practice but the essence of the reporting process remains the same as others discussed in this chapter. Comments written in the report should be objective, based upon evidence which has been documented in the teacher records and should be appropriately referenced (i.e. criterion, ipsative or norm). For an external audience some indication of the context of learning may be appropriate. The report should identify the pupil's strengths and weaknesses and the extent to which targets have been achieved, and indicate the amount and nature of support which the pupil has received.

5.11 How can pupils be involved in reporting?

Pupils can be involved in reporting to each of the three audiences identified in this chapter. Their main involvement is in the formative assessment process, with the guidance of the teacher. Pupils can be involved in formative reporting to their parents and next teacher and within summative reporting to external professional audiences.

Many of the skills employed in oral reporting can be developed through circle time (Bliss 1994) where cognitive, affective and conative pupil responses are sought. Pupils are encouraged to listen to others, to take turns, to structure their own responses and to ask questions. Circle time is an appropriate introduction to sharing work with peers, teachers and parents, both informally and formally.

Individual pupil–teacher conferences, or reviews, provide an opportunity for the teacher to enter into dialogue with individual pupils using their work from exercise books, folders or the Individual Pupil Portfolio to stimulate recall of the learning undertaken. The teacher works with pupils to help identify and analyse cognitive strengths and weaknesses. Pupils provide additional affective and conative information, enabling the teacher to learn more about their individual needs. Together the pupil and teacher decide upon the most important areas for development and determine appropriate and challenging targets.

Within a review situation the teacher provides 'metacognitive guidance' (Nisbet and Shucksmith 1986) and 'scaffolded support' (Ashman and Conway 1997) by modelling lower and higher order questions which pupils will need to use in self-assessment. The teacher provides the pupil with a metacognitive model as she probes not just the content of the pupils' learning but their preferred styles of learning and why some learning is more effective for individuals than others.

✎ ACTIVITY 5.5

Interview three pupils individually about their learning in writing. Have a range of the pupil's work available for reference purposes at each interview. Try to find out how aware the pupils are of their strengths and weaknesses. Ask the pupils to determine three targets for their learning. What support did the pupils need when analysing their work? Share and discuss your findings with their teacher.

Pupils can be involved in the statutory oral and written reporting to parents in several ways. Some schools provide an opportunity during the year for a three-way discussion between pupil, parent and teacher to discuss the pupil's progress and to set targets which have been agreed by all parties. If pupils are not invited to the parent–teacher consultation they can be involved in choosing or highlighting the work which they would like their parents to see and which, in their view, demonstrates key features of their learning. This is more effective if pupils have annotated their work in some way to alert their parents to the key features. This could be developed through the year or Key Stage as an Individual Pupil Portfolio or Record of Achievement, which in itself provides a useful formative assessment experience for the pupils (see Chapter 4). Finally, in some schools pupils may be asked to add their own comments on written reports to parents, taking greater involvement within the formal reporting process.

Pupil involvement in reporting to the next teacher when moving during the school year can include the selection of work and a commentary to demonstrate strengths, weaknesses and learning targets. When moving from primary to secondary schools this can be less useful for the receiving teacher (McCallum 1996). Some innovative practices, such as a desktop published curriculum vitae with an attached photograph and personal targets, demonstrate the pupils' abilities in self-assessment when reporting to a new school where transfer documentation must be kept to a minimum.

5.12 Case studies in reporting

CASE STUDY 5.1

Gemma was a PGCE trainee on her final block practice at a large urban infant school. She had taken the class of 28 spring and summer entry reception children for approximately 0.8 of the week during most of the practice. Gemma had initially worked alongside the class teacher on Baseline Assessment activities and maintained purposeful records on all the children throughout the seven week practice.

Gemma's class teacher, Mrs Jones, was also the deputy head teacher and was frequently called away to cover for the head teacher, initially for meetings and then for long-term sick leave. A supply teacher worked with Gemma and other teachers in the year group, offering practical and moral support.

Gemma enjoyed taking class responsibility and the children were positive in their response to her as the teacher. The 'summer entry' children and their parents had more contact during the term with Gemma than Mrs Jones but Mrs Jones recognised her responsibility for end of year reports and parents' evening. Three weeks before the end of the practice she set up a series of after school meetings with Gemma to discuss the report writing requirements of the school in terms of content, length and style. At Mrs Jones' request, Gemma identified ten children and used her assessment notes to write reports in the house style. They discussed the reports and Gemma then wrote and submitted ten more. Gemma realised that she would need to undertake more detailed assessments before writing reports for the final eight children as her notes provided overview comments rather than precise remarks. She restructured her classroom practice accordingly.

- How could Gemma use her experience of Baseline Assessment in writing reports to parents?

- How can records which contain purposeful formative comments be used to write a summative report?

- How should Gemma build upon her reporting practice as an NQT?

CASE STUDY 5.2

Julie was an NQT teaching 27 Y2 pupils in a small primary school in a village location. The school had been using a home–school mathematics project for two years. A mathematics activity, for pupils to undertake with their parents in the home environment, was given every two weeks. The work was followed up in class. Pupils, parents and teachers were asked to complete a section in the pupil's mathematics diary to track progress and response.

Julie was initially daunted by the prospect of writing comments to parents. The Y1 teacher showed her some examples of diary comments from the previous year and discussed the range of communication he had experienced. Julie also began to meet and speak with parents as they brought and collected their children from school.

She decided simply to respond to the remarks made by pupils and parents in the diary. Julie soon realised the diary provided a useful informal dialogue between home and school and provided a further insight to the pupil's mathematics learning.

● What are the differences in style and approach between writing comments in a subject diary and an annual written report?

● Should Julie simply respond to comments made by pupils and parents?

● How could a subject diary enhance home–school communication?

CHAPTER 6

Accountability

In 1976 Prime Minister Callaghan ... suggested that education should be more accountable to society and that a general consideration of educational issues should be opened up to give non-professionals a chance to have their say.

(Gipps and Goldstein 1983)

6.1 What is accountability?

Accountability is a term which provides for the last of the four purposes of assessment identified by TGAT (DES 1988), 'evaluative'. The document stated that there should be a means by which 'some aspects of the work of a school, an LEA or other discrete part of the educational service can be assessed and/or reported upon' (para. 23). Since the report was published a variety of systems and structures have been developed to ensure the accountability of education and much has rested upon the quantitative data generated by National Curriculum Assessment.

Accountability has moral, legal and financial dimensions and operates at all levels of the education system. Teachers have a moral and legal responsibility to provide appropriate educational experiences for pupils and to report to parents and other professionals. The head teacher and governing body have a legal responsibility to ensure the finances of the school are used effectively to benefit pupils' education. The school is answerable to the LEA and DfES. The Secretary of State for Education is responsible for providing financial resources and ensuring their use in a manner which will enhance educational provision. He is assisted by organisations such as QCA and TTA which provide specific support for different parts of the education system. HMI and OFSTED oversee the quality of teaching and learning through inspection.

6.2 To whom are teachers accountable?

Teachers are, first and foremost, accountable to their pupils. They are responsible for providing work which is interesting and challenging, maintaining pupils' involvement and helping them make progress in their learning. Teachers are accountable to pupils on a daily basis, in and beyond lessons.

Secondly, teachers are accountable to parents, both legally and morally, for the educational development of their children. The most evident mechanism for this is through the formal reporting channels (see Chapter 5) and through the provision of information about pupils' progress whenever necessary.

Thirdly, teachers are accountable to their fellow professionals, in and beyond the school, through the provision of accurate and appropriate information from which pupils' educational progress can be tracked, measured and compared. To ensure the reliability of this information teachers should be willing to participate in activities and discussion which develops shared professional understanding and enhances good practice. Teachers are accountable to fellow professionals in the LEA and DfES, to share statistical information on pupils' progress and to become involved in initiatives designed to improve the quality of learning provision for pupils.

Ultimately, teachers are accountable to taxpayers. Without taxpayers' money the national system of schooling would disintegrate. Public funds must be seen to be delivering value for money. The general public are kept informed about the quality of schooling their money buys through two main sources. Firstly, OFSTED reports provide details of individual school inspections and collated evidence, concerning subjects and particular educational issues, are brought together through specific reports and the Annual Report of the Chief HMI. Secondly, the publication of performance tables charts the results at the end of Key Stages 2 and 3, GCSE and A-level. OFSTED reports and performance tables are available through libraries and the internet (www.ofsted.gov.uk), and the national and local media provide information and interpretation based upon these two main sources.

6.3 Why is there a need for accountability?

Accountability is not new. As far back as the 1830s when public money was used to establish a national education system 'some [MPs] were concerned that the spending of public money should be properly supervised and controlled, and others were dissatisfied with the practical aspects such as the poor quality of the teachers' (Lawton and Gordon 1987, p. 7). This led to the formation of an inspectorate to monitor financial provision to schools. It initially comprised not teachers but those who 'had followed careers in the church, university or in law'

(Lawton and Gordon 1987, p. 10). By 1862, inspectors used the Revised Code of six standards upon which to base their judgements of schools (see Chapter 2, section 2.5).

In more recent times the need for accountability can be seen in three broad stages each with particular incidents which focused upon accountability to pupils, parents, the government and the wider public.

The first stage saw for many, though not all, the beginning of comprehensive secondary education and the end of the selective education system which had been set up under the tripartite system of the 1944 Education Act. Comprehensive education impacted on primary schools which, free of the 11+ with its emphasis upon English and mathematics, could embrace a wider curriculum and the progressive, child-centred education of the Plowden Report (Plowden 1967). But public concern about the growth and nature of progressive education was fuelled by an occurrence in 1975 at William Tyndale Junior School in Islington, when parents complained about the quality of their children's education. This led to a public enquiry, the dismissal of the head teacher and several staff, and the publication of the Auld Report (Gipps and Goldstein 1983). The following year in his speech at Ruskin College, Oxford, the Prime Minister James Callaghan stated that education should be more accountable and he initiated a period of public discussion which became known as 'The Great Debate'. The Conservative government which came to power in 1979 developed the notion of accountability further still. Legislative changes throughout the 1980s made schools more accountable to parents and the community through the provision of information and representation on governing bodies.

The second stage saw the introduction and development of the 1988 Education Reform Act with the National Curriculum, its assessment and the opportunity for parents to decide whether schools should move away from the LEA to become Grant Maintained (Maclure 1992). The five key documents of *The Parent's Charter* (see Figure 6.1) indicated the information which schools were to provide to become more accountable to their parent-clients in the new age of market forces (Bridges 1994; Headington and Howson 1995; James and Phillips 1995) and set the agenda for further legislation to enforce them.

- A report about your child
- Regular reports from independent inspectors
- Performance tables for all your local schools
- A prospectus or brochure about individual schools
- An annual report from your school governors

Figure 6.1 The five key documents (from DES 1991b)

> ✎ ACTIVITY **6.1**
>
> Interview parents to discover the extent to which the information provided within each of the five key documents helps them to gain an understanding of their children's education and the work of the school. Compare your findings with colleagues.

The third stage saw the New Labour government come to power in 1997 with the rallying cry of 'Education! Education! Education!'. The government aimed to 'raise standards' and supported techniques used in the business world, such as data analysis and target setting. The growth of education data, based mainly upon OFSTED reports and National Curriculum performance details, along with the growth of information and communication technology, enhanced the possibility of using business models. Terms such as value added, benchmarking and target setting, once an anathema to education, became common parlance. Education was seen as a vehicle for social and economic development and everyone, from the Secretary of State to the individual pupil, was seen as having a duty to improve standards of performance, to be accountable to the country in order to enhance both national and international status.

6.4 What is a standard?

Standards have been referred to frequently in the world of education. Concern that 'standards have fallen' and that 'standards need to improve' has dominated political debate for well over a hundred years. But what is a standard and how can it fall or improve?

A standard is an expected level of performance. Standards are set at the levels considered appropriate at that time. The performance of Year 6 pupils either reach, exceed or fall short of the Level 4 standard in the National Curriculum assessments in English, mathematics and science. Standards do not change, but performance does. This is evident in athletics where each year previous records are broken and athletes reach still higher expected levels of performance. New standards are set as overall performance improves.

It follows that 'declining standards' occur when '*performance* is not coming up to standard to the extent that it once did or that performance is coming up to a standard which is different from that which once it came up to – and different in the sense that it is less demanding than the other standards' (Pring 1996, p. 15).

'Raising standards' requires average performance to improve to such an extent that new, higher, standards can be set. In National Curriculum terms the expectation is that average pupils will reach Level 2 at age 7 and Level 4 at age 11. The percentage of pupils expected to be 'average' provides evidence to support the standard in place at that time. When this figure was examined in 1997 by the incoming government, the percentage of pupils with 'average' performance was deemed to be too low. It was decided to improve average performance by setting

national targets for literacy and numeracy at Key Stage 2 ... that, by 2002:

- 80 per cent of 11 year olds will reach Level 4 in English; and
- 75 per cent of 11 year olds will reach Level 4 in mathematics. (DfEE 1997b)

Although these targets were not met by 2002, there was a substantial increase in performance across the country. Standards had been raised. New targets were set to improve performance still further.

6.5 What sources of evidence are available to the general public?

Two sources of accountability evidence which are available to the general public are OFSTED inspection reports and performance tables. Both are national, statutory, easily accessible and well publicised by the media. Both enable the general public to draw opinions about the quality of educational provision within an individual school and to make comparisons between schools. Both overtly influence the daily lives of teachers and their pupils.

- through informal comments by parents; and,
- through research.'

How is the quality of schooling monitored through informal comments by parents and through research? Why may these areas appear less influential to the daily lives of teachers and their pupils than inspection reports and published test results? Should this be the case?

OFSTED inspections provide a first source of data to the general public. OFSTED developed from HMI following the 1992 Education Act. No part of the national education system escapes inspection. Nurseries, schools, LEAs and teacher training courses are all inspected and the reports, focusing upon the quality of teaching and learning within the institution, are made public.

School inspections take place regularly, when trained teams of inspectors, including educationalists and a lay member, are contracted to visit individual schools for about a week, depending upon the size and composition of the school and the team. The inspection evidence base comprises data from observations, interviews, a questionnaire for and meeting with parents and analysis of pupils' work, school policies and summary data. It culminates in an inspection report which is accessible to the general public.

✎ ACTIVITY 6.2

Access, from the Ofsted website (www.ofsted.gov.uk), the most recent inspection report for a school with which you are familiar. Skim read the report for the main findings, points for action, section headings and statistical information. Read in detail the sections on English and mathematics, one of the foundation subjects and assessment. To what extent does the report confirm your impression of the teaching and learning within the school? How accessible is the content, style and language of the report to a diverse public audience (see Chapter 5, section 5.2)?

OFSTED handbooks provide the criteria for inspection and as institutions have become more familiar with the inspection process and more conversant with the demands made, many have adopted systems to monitor effectiveness between inspections. This includes monitoring of planning and teaching and using assessment data to analyse and consider how to improve the quality of teaching and learning.

Primary School Performance Tables of Key Stage 2 Results provide a second source of data to the general public. They reflect the work of the whole school, not just one teacher. Practising for the 11+ was once left to the Year 6 teacher, but as the 'high stakes' nature of End of Key Stage tests has grown it has been accepted that pupils cannot achieve a Level 4 overnight, that practice throughout the school can, in most cases, influence summative results. This effect is known as 'washback'. Teachers and pupils have become more familiar with the content and style of National Curriculum tests through the use of QCA Optional Tests. The statistics which these and other assessments provide help the head teacher and staff to monitor the performance of individual pupils, classes and cohorts, to predict their results in future years and to target particular aspects of their learning.

The publication of Primary School Performance Tables of Key Stage 2 Results was initially viewed with suspicion. The media declared them to be 'league tables' through which schools should be compared for quality of educational provision and proceeded to name schools which had gained the highest and lowest results. This practice was condemned by many in the education community. Mortimore (1996, p. 22), for example, declared that 'league tables of...pupils' results can say little about the quality of schooling: they provide, instead, a good indication of the background and amount of prior learning of pupils'. The inclusion of information such as the percentage of pupils who were absent or disapplied from the tests, the number of pupils deemed to have special educational needs, and the number with and without statements, has helped to bridge the gap between the presentation of raw data and that which provides some explanation. The inclusion of an average percentage score of the three core subjects across several years may provide the lay person with a more immediate reference point to determine whether performance has improved in a school, LEA or nationally. However, concern has been raised that performance tables show the levels attained rather than the progress pupils have made. Information which indicates progress rather than attainment has been considered as more appropriate.

✎ ACTIVITY 6.3

Examine results from an LEA's Primary School Performance Tables of Key Stage 2 Results (www.dfes.gov.uk/performancetables). Working with one or two others write up to five questions which arise from the statistics. For example:

- Why did the average point score of School A rise from last year when the score of School B stayed at a similar level?
- Although they achieved similar results was School C 'better' than School D as it entered more pupils for the tests?
- Do schools with high proportions of pupils with special educational needs necessarily have weaker results?

Exchange questions with others who have undertaken this exercise. Answer their questions. Discuss the outcomes of the exercise as a large group.

6.6 What is value added?

Value added is a measure which shows the progress made by pupils from one stage to the next. When performance tables were first published there was concern that the results of different schools would not reflect the amount of work or the socio-economic circumstances of the pupils. Two schools could both have 65 per cent of pupils reaching Level 4 and above in English and no distinction would be apparent between pupils who had made little progress through their primary years and those who had worked against the odds to meet the same figure.

Tymms (1999, p. 59) described the term 'value added' as 'very unfortunate. It has two quite different meanings and this causes considerable difficulties that lead to confusion.' The first and more simplistic approach to value added rests on using the numerical difference between the results at Key Stage 1 and at Key Stage 2.

✎ ACTIVITY 6.4

Examine the Key Stage 1 and Key Stage 2 tests. List the similarities and differences between their structure, content, administration and marking. Consider whether a simple comparison can be made between the two.

This approach was not deemed appropriate as the assessments made at Baseline, Key Stage 1 and Key Stage 2 were not comparable in content or technical accuracy in areas such as validity and reliability (Lindsay and Desforges 1998; Shorrocks-Taylor 1999). The simplistic approach was also fraught with difficulties, such as the ever changing population of the school (Tymms and Henderson 1996). Like could not be compared with like with such ease.

A second and more technical approach to using value added measures in the primary school was investigated within The Value Added National Project (Tymms and Henderson 1996) and was adopted within the 2002 KS1–KS2 Value Added Pilot (www.dfes.gov.uk/performancetables). This approach was based on how pupils progress in relation to other pupils. A pupil's score was compared with the median performance of other pupils with the same or similar KS1 attainment. Sometimes the value added was positive and sometimes it was negative. The approach was more statistically valid than the simplistic approach described previously but it too had difficulties. It required accurate information of individual pupils' results based upon comparable assessments and a large enough sample size to ensure that measurements were statistically valid (Tymms and Henderson 1996). The pilot recognised the need to include statistics on coverage, the number of pupils included in the measure, and stability, the percentage of pupils included within the same school at both Key Stages. Tymms (1999) provided an accessible and informative explanation of value added, the measurement of residuals.

The use of information technology has made the development of value added more feasible but the complexity of the measure cannot be denied. The difficulty of explaining information that accurately reflects the progress in pupils' learning has appeared to outweigh the public's need for this information. The raw data of summative assessment has instead been left for public scrutiny and interpretation. Value added data has instead been recommended for use in schools as a means of analysing and comparing pupils' progress from Key Stage 1 to Key Stage 2 (DfEE 1999d).

6.7 What is comparative data?

Since the 1988 Education Reform Act introduced the use of National Curriculum levels to demonstrate attainment, numbers have become the currency of education and data analysis in relation to teaching and learning has become an expectation. The fast-growing information and communication technology has provided a vehicle for collecting and representing statistics, enabling large quantities of information to be interpreted and analysed. The cumulative data of several years of National Curriculum Assessment results at national, local and school level has enabled organisations at different levels to monitor their own progress, notice trends and predict future outcomes based upon previous experience. At a macro-level, quantitative data has provided evidence for phenomena which had previously rested in teacher mythology, such as the attainment 'dip' as pupils move into Key Stage 3 (Pollitt 2000). At a micro-level, quantitative data has provided evidence of the progress and learning of individual pupils which, with the teacher's personal knowledge of the pupil's circumstances, has been used to help determine individual pupil targets.

Such data analysis requires a sense of number and some understanding of statistics, areas that must now be demonstrated through the numeracy skills test by those who wish to gain Qualified Teacher Status.

Primary schools experienced an upsurge in data collection from 1997 but, as a result, were provided by their LEAs with an annual analysis of their own data in comparison with all schools within the LEA and with other schools with similar characteristics in 'PandAs' (Performance and Assessment Data) and 'Autumn Packages' (see www.standards.dfes.gov.uk/performance/ap). While data analysis has generally been the preserve of senior management and the governing body, Pollard (2002, p. 334) noted that the introduction of Performance Management 'has been the spur for many teachers to get to grips with the Autumn Package'.

The grouping of schools into 'clusters', using contextualised information such as the percentages of pupils entitled to free school meals and those with similar aggregated Key Stage 1 results, enabled schools to match like-with-like in respect of their pupils' performance. This has provided schools with 'benchmarks' against which to measure the performance of their pupils.

Within the analysis, schools were given 'benchmark tables' of national, local and cluster group results using quartile tables. These are formed by placing the results of several schools in order and identifying the result which is at the middle point or median, the 75th percentile or upper quartile and the 25th percentile or lower quartile (see Table 6.1). Further percentiles, such as the 95th, can be given to provide greater detail (see Table 6.2).

The figures used in Tables 6.1 and 6.2 represent percentages of pupils attaining Level 4 and above in End of Key Stage 2 National Curriculum tests, providing a direct link with performance tables. An alternative method of representing data in PandAs is to give the average National Curriculum levels achieved by pupils within the school. As Level 4 is the expected level at age 11, a figure of 3.5, for example, would signify underachievement (SCAA 1997e).

Table 6.1 Making a quartile table

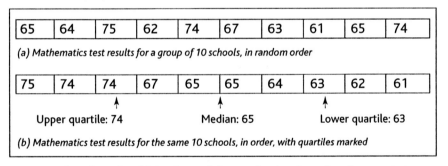

65	64	75	62	74	67	63	61	65	74

(a) Mathematics test results for a group of 10 schools, in random order

75	74	74	67	65	65	64	63	62	61

Upper quartile: 74   Median: 65   Lower quartile: 63

(b) Mathematics test results for the same 10 schools, in order, with quartiles marked

Once a 'benchmark table' is formed from schools of similar characteristics, an individual school can see its results in relation to others. In Table 6.2 two schools within the same cluster group are identified as being higher and lower than the median. This gives an immediate impression of the school's position within the cluster group, but it is equally important to know how the cluster group compares with others locally and nationally.

To make comparisons more straightforward to interpret, grades with descriptive statements are also provided within the PandA. An example of the grading of School C is given in Table 6.3. Grade B means pupils' results are above the national average/average for similar schools. Grade C means pupils' results are broadly in line with the national average/average for similar schools. Grade D means pupils' results are below the national average/average for similar schools.

Table 6.2 Benchmark tables

	95th percentile	Upper quartile	School A	Median	Lower quartile
English	78	75	70	69	64
Mathematics	75	74	68	65	63
Science	78	76	72	70	68
Averages	77	75	70	68	65

(a) School A results highlighted within the benchmark table of 10 schools

	95th percentile	Upper quartile	Median	School B	Lower quartile
English	78	75	69	66	64
Mathematics	75	74	65	64	63
Science	78	76	70	68	68
Averages	77	75	68	66	65

(b) School B results highlighted within the benchmark table of 10 schools

Table 6.3 Grades based upon NC levels for School C

	In comparison with all LEA schools	In comparison with similar schools
English	C	B
Mathematics	D	C
Science	C	B

Discussion 6.3

What can you discover about the pupils' results in Schools A, B and C from the tables given? How could the national and local comparative data assist in the development of teaching and learning within individual schools?

Comparative data provide the individual school with an indication of its pupils' progress in relation to other schools. As this information is provided annually the school can remain alert to its current position against similar schools, other LEA schools and nationally, and so set realistic school targets. While useful in many respects the use of National Curriculum Assessment data for such comparisons is not without its critics (Richards 2001).

6.8 What is target setting?

Target setting is part of an improvement plan. The government brought target setting into education from a business perspective to help structure school improvement. When an organisation realises its own position and its position in comparison with others, it can work to improve upon this by deciding upon a goal to work towards, by setting a target, and putting into action a means by which to meet the target.

But target setting can be used at a number of different levels. It has always been at the heart of good practice in assessment. It is the 'desired goal' referred to by Sadler (1989), who recognised the need for evidence to determine the 'present position' and an understanding of how to 'close the gap' between the two. Target setting must necessarily lead to action by pupil and teacher, an area discussed further in section 6.9.

As mentioned in section 6.4, in 1997 the government set national targets for 11 year olds to reach in 2002. This set into motion a cascade of target setting throughout the education system, where each stratum endeavoured to help the next to reach its targets. LEAs set their targets in consultation with the DfEE/DfES. Individual schools set their targets in consultation with the LEA. Class targets and individual pupil targets were set by school senior management teams and class teachers. The target setting model used was 'top-down' and based solely upon those parts of English and mathematics which were deemed measurable. It focused upon quantitative data rather than qualitative approaches to learning even though the performance of individual pupils was central to national target setting.

Circular 11/98 (DfEE 1998c) gave statutory requirements for target setting in schools and stated that 'Target setting has been shown in research and inspection evidence to help raise standards of pupil performance'. The booklet From Targets to Action (DfEE 1997b) had already set out five stages in the cycle of school improvement.

The school:

- Stage 1: analyses its current performance
- Stage 2: compares its results with those of similar schools
- Stage 3: sets itself clear and measurable targets
- Stage 4: revises its development plan to highlight action to achieve the targets
- Stage 5: takes action, reviews, success, and starts the cycle again.

It stated that targets 'must be set in terms of pupils' performance in National Curriculum assessments' and encouraged the use of SMART targets which are Specific, Measurable, Achievable, Realistic and Time-related. To emphasise the need for 'challenging yet realistic targets' four progressive Target Zones were described as

- The Historic Zone
- The Comfort Zone
- The Challenge Zone
- The Unlikely Zone

with current performance being on the cusp of the historic and comfort zone. The booklet emphasised the need for an evidence base upon which to base school target setting and identified the four sources of

- the school's record of past performance;
- national and LEA benchmark information about the performance of similar schools;
- information about the rate of progress needed to achieve national and LEA targets; and
- teachers' forecasts of pupil performance in forthcoming years.

The action necessary to achieve school targets recommended 'changes in classroom practice [with] concerted effort over time'.

There have been noticeable changes in classroom practice since the inception of target setting practice in schools. Teachers have become more aware of their pupils' progress through the National Curriculum levels and have experienced 'washback' from higher year groups, with emphasis on the core curriculum subjects (McNess 2001). In Year 6 'targeting' of individual pupils in particular areas of weakness has taken place, particularly if the performance of these pupils straddles the border of two levels. Booster classes have been encouraged and financed by the government to help the most able Year 6 pupils achieve even better results. Summer schools have also been financed to provide additional support to weaker pupils during the long break when so many have fallen further behind. Homework has been encouraged and homework clubs have gathered momentum to allow those pupils without suitable facilities to undertake work in school at lunchtime or after school hours. And the National Literacy and National Numeracy Strategies have influenced the nature and duration of work in English and mathematics. And, in the two subjects at the centre of the target setting process, National Curriculum tests have developed accordingly.

Discussion 6.4

In an interview on Radio 4 (BBC 2003), the former Secretary of State for Education, Estelle Morris, said that while targets set by oneself are generally perceived as empowering, targets set by others are often perceived as punitive. Discuss with colleagues your experiences of target setting in schools. Was the government right in leading the target setting process?

Is this model of target setting a 'professional monitoring system' or an 'official accountability system' (Tymms 1998, p. 56)?

6.9 How can pupils be involved in accountability?

Pupils are accountable to themselves, their parents, their peers and teachers. Accountability provides an opportunity for individuals to develop within a supportive network.

Pupils can be encouraged to be accountable to themselves by undertaking self-assessment, by setting challenging yet realistic personal targets, by tracking targets and asking for assistance in reaching them. The skills and strategies discussed in previous chapters enable pupils to engage in this process with confidence, share their progress with parents, peers and teachers and encourage other pupils.

They may also be involved in other levels of accountability within the school. Teachers may wish to find out more about the pupils' reaction to initiatives, such as the National Literacy Strategy and National Numeracy Strategy, and particular circumstances, such as bullying, through surveys to improve teaching provision and pastoral care within the school. Pupils may be asked to represent their class on the school's council to discuss the provision of homework clubs or to represent their school in a sporting event. They may be asked to assist in open days and promote the work of the school in art or drama, or guide a potential parent around the school, answering questions courteously and honestly.

All of these areas, whether they are directly related to learning or not, provide pupils with experiences of accountability to themselves and to others which they will build upon as they grow older.

6.10 Case studies in accountability

CASE STUDY 6.1

Nick was a PGCE trainee undertaking his first block practice at an 8–12 urban middle school which had three classes in each year group. Nick took a Y5 class of 32 pupils. He was required to teach all areas of the curriculum although he had spent the previous three years studying for a history degree.

On her first visit the College Tutor told Nick that his file needed greater consideration. Learning objectives were appropriate but there was insufficient detail about the content, presentation and organisation of the lessons. The comments made about individual pupils lacked purpose and dealt with the work covered rather than assessing the quality of response. This was in stark contrast to his practice, which the College Tutor praised. In class he was well organised and had clear expectations of the lesson development and of the pupils' learning and behaviour. He had worked with the class to produce an interactive display on dental hygiene and was becoming actively involved in lunchtime sports clubs.

After discussion it emerged that Nick saw the file as a time consuming document written for others rather than as a useful working document. He kept a separate notebook of working notes, ideas and organisational points. Nick decided to bring the two documents together. He increased the level of detail in his lesson plans and this in turn meant he did not need to provide descriptive detail in the assessment records. Instead he focused upon analysing the learning which had taken place against the objectives he had identified and recognised how this would inform his future planning.

- Were the file and record keeping demands of the college in opposition to Nick's needs as a trainee teacher?

- Why might the College Tutor have insisted upon file changes although Nick's practice appeared satisfactory?

- What advice on file and record keeping would you give Nick for his final practice?

CASE STUDY 6.2

Chris was about to start as an NQT at an urban 4–11 primary school which had some major areas of concern in a recent OFSTED inspection. She was to teach a Y3 class of 30 pupils. At the end of July Chris asked the head teacher for any relevant records from which she could gain an awareness of the pupils' abilities and so begin to plan for the Autumn Term. She knew there would be information from the End of Key Stage One Tests and Teacher Assessments and hoped for additional information such as reading ages and general comments from the previous teacher.

Chris was told that the Y2 teacher had left the school and that no records existed other than the numerical data which had been statutorily reported to parents at the end of the Key Stage. Children had also been allowed to take home their KS1 workbooks. Chris was given a list of pupils' names with NCA and TA levels and the comparative data which had been provided for parents at the end of the previous school year.

- What information is available to Chris?

- How should Chris use the End of Key Stage results to best advantage?

- What assessments would Chris need to prioritise in the first weeks of the school year to discover more about the pupils' learning and learning needs?

CHAPTER 7

Moving forward with MARRA

Assessment must work for children.

(Drummond 1993)

7.1 Why are there standards in MARRA?

The standards documented in the Professional Standards for Qualified Teacher Status, and the Induction Standards for Newly Qualified Teachers, encapsulate the most important areas in which trainee teachers and NQTs must be proficient to become competent practitioners. They must be aware of their professional responsibilities, have a good knowledge and understanding of what and who they are to teach, be able to plan for the needs of all pupils, use monitoring and assessment effectively and be able to manage the learning environment and teach pupils using a range of strategies.

MARRA is a linchpin within this array of standards. It is a combination of interrelated assessment issues, all of which have a direct relationship with pupils' learning. MARRA requires a critical awareness of the theory upon which assessment practice is based. It requires the ability to operate effectively at many different levels, from close diagnostic work with an individual pupil to recognising how targets are used to improve national results in literacy and numeracy. It requires the ability to work with a range of personnel, from pupils and LSAs to governors and parents. It requires a recognition of the roles and responsibilities of others within the education system, from the school senior management team to the Secretary of State for Education. It requires an awareness of the importance of MARRA to people at different levels of the education system, including politicians and policy makers, LEAs and schools, parents and teachers. It requires the ability to use assessment to improve the quality of teaching and an understanding of the centrality of pupils in the assessment process.

7.2 Why is MARRA important to politicians and policy makers?

Politicians and policy makers have had a considerable impact upon MARRA since the 1980s. A plethora of education legislation and guidance has brought into being centralised systems and structures, regulations and responsibilities. Vast sums of money have been spent putting legislation and guidance into action. Legislation has focused upon curriculum content and its assessment. It has required open access to information about pupils' performance and has enhanced parents' rights. Guidance has helped teachers to interpret the published curriculum and recognise the requirements of associated statutory assessment. It has recommended lesson structures in the key areas of literacy and numeracy and planning frameworks in other curriculum areas. Together legislation and guidance have informed teachers of *what* they must teach, recommended *how* it should be taught and have enabled these areas to be monitored nationally through statutory assessment and inspection.

Technology has aided the collection, interrogation and dissemination of data from statutory assessment. Politicians and policy makers use the data, based increasingly upon the specific and measurable areas of reading, writing and number, to evaluate the quality of education available and to make comparisons with other countries. Successive governments have looked to models from business and industry to determine how 'higher standards' can be achieved in education. By deciding where and how to spend financial resources, governments have highlighted the areas of education which they considered to be most important. For example, national targets and a greater emphasis upon literacy and numeracy through national strategy initiatives, along with booster classes for more able pupils, summer schools for those who need time to 'catch up' with their peers and homework for all, followed research and international comparison which suggested that levels of literacy and numeracy were insufficient (OFSTED 1996b; Reynolds and Farrell 1996).

Government spending on resources and initiatives is evaluated in terms of its value for money and provides politicians and policy makers with accountability evidence, demonstrating the effectiveness of their strategies to the taxpayers who ultimately pay for the education service.

7.3 Why is MARRA important to LEAs and schools?

LEAs and schools work together to manage government resources and initiatives in practice. They use MARRA to determine how financial and practical resources should be allocated to benefit pupils and schools. Results of summative statutory assessments are used to monitor trends and inconsistencies and to target areas of need.

LEA advisory and inspection services work with schools to develop and implement OFSTED action plans and School Development Plans. For example, if in-service training is required upon specific aspects of curriculum, such as mental mathematics, LEA advisory staff may work in the school, with some or all members of staff, or they may run LEA courses to address particular needs. Similarly LEA specialists work with SENCOs to devise and implement statements of special educational need for individual pupils, and they support additional provision for pupils with EAL and those who are gifted and talented.

LEAs often run training courses for teachers in statutory assessment and related areas of professional development such as transfer, moderation and involving pupils in self-assessment. LEA personnel are involved in audits during the statutory assessment period, checking that administration arrangements have been carried out satisfactorily and processing optical mark reader sheets at Key Stage 1. They may be invited into schools to explain elements of the statutory assessment process and the use of comparative results, to staff or to parents.

Schools use statutory assessment results to monitor the progress of groups and individual pupils. They compare the results of their own school with others of a similar nature, to determine whether the school targets they have set are realistic and challenging. They monitor the progress of groups of pupils and subject areas to determine whether different approaches to teaching and learning, such as setting by ability in mathematics, may be more effective. They use cumulative data to track and predict the progress of individual pupils, target their learning needs and provide appropriate support.

Schools also keep parents informed of the progress of their own children in relation to the age group within the school and nationally. They work with parents to explore and monitor contributory factors, including the social, physical and emotional, which may affect a pupil's academic progress, seeking the assistance of outside agencies such as Social Services where necessary.

7.4 Why is MARRA important to parents and teachers?

Parents and teachers use MARRA to ensure the progress of individual pupils. Parents can monitor the progress of their children in relation to previous past performance in the Foundation Stage Profile and End of Key Stage tests. They can use the criteria of the National Curriculum document to identify what their children know, do and understand in relation to the levels of attainment. They can compare their children with the performance of other children of the same age at the school and with others of the same age nationally. They can discuss their children's progress with the class teacher and, with her and the children, determine appropriate targets and how they can help in the learning process.

MARRA encourages teachers to monitor and assess the learning and learning needs of all the pupils in a class as a complementary part of the planning and assessment cycles. The processes of recording and reporting ensure regular and objective approaches are developed and maintained and these in turn enable accountability to pupils, parents and professionals. Teachers use formative and diagnostic assessment to make the work undertaken with pupils more appropriate to their learning needs. They use summative assessments to bring together many aspects of pupils' learning and to report to others. They use summative assessments from other teachers to develop learning programmes for new pupils.

The assessments which teachers undertake with individual pupils are central to MARRA. Formative and diagnostic assessment impacts directly upon pupils' learning; it leads towards summative assessment which in turn enables evaluative assessment. Teachers' work with individual pupils is pivotal to school, LEA and national systems and structures such as reaching literacy and numeracy targets and 'raising standards'. One of the most beneficial steps which a teacher can take to enhance assessment and learning is to involve pupils in MARRA.

7.5 How can pupils be involved in MARRA?

Pupils can be involved in every aspect of MARRA, becoming actively engaged in the learning process and becoming aware of their learning strategies and thinking processes with the teachers' help and guidance. The teacher can assist pupils by sharing or negotiating learning objectives with them in language they will understand and providing lesson structures which encourage pupils to plan, do and review their learning. She can encourage pupils to develop and meet personal learning targets based upon self-assessment. The teacher can encourage pupils to build a record of their progress in learning and assess what they have learned, how they have learned and why they have learned. She can make links between different areas of the curriculum to demonstrate the transferable nature of metacognition and to encourage cognitive, affective and conative responses to learning.

The teacher who models and encourages reflective practice helps her pupils to approach learning in a more reflective manner. She encourages pupils to identify and build upon their success. She encourages them to respond positively to situations which are more demanding by breaking them down into smaller, more manageable steps. She encourages them to look for information and strategies across different aspects of learning, to recognise patterns and make connections. If MARRA is used effectively it must benefit pupils' learning by engaging pupils with their learning. Figure 7.1 demonstrates how this was achieved with the same four pupils who featured in Chapter 1.

113

Wesley enjoyed the oral mental arithmetic game he played with the teacher. He became more accurate in his mental addition, gradually improved the speed at which he could work and, to his delight, regularly beat the teacher. Wesley's success in the activity empowered him as he became more actively engaged in whole-class mental arithmetic sessions. He asked the teacher if they could use 'harder numbers to 20'. Wesley had self-assessed, developed and set a new target for himself.

Heidi's experience of shared reading with the teacher motivated her to work with another pupil of similar reading ability. They chose the same books, read together at various points during the day, both in and out of lesson time, and agreed how much to read at home. Heidi also chose to follow the text of books as she listened to story tapes. Some weeks later she commented to the teacher that 'the punctuation tells you how to read aloud'. As Heidi had read and heard a variety of texts she had noticed patterns which could be applied to new situations.

Ricky worked with a partner to write a story for pupils in a Y2 class, in which both had siblings. They chose a setting and characters before deciding what would happen in the story and how it would end. They considered whether the vocabulary list they had generated would be appropriate for the intended audience. Ricky suggested that cartoons would be a useful way of telling the story, to engage the audience and to introduce words which might be new. He had reviewed his own learning strategies and considered how they could relate to the learning of others.

Angela and her teacher reviewed her work to choose new items for her Individual Pupil Portfolio prior to the Spring Term parents' evening. Together they looked through Angela's written work in English. At the beginning of the year the teacher had underlined many spelling errors. From the point at which Angela had begun to use 'checklists' significant differences were apparent. Angela remarked that there were fewer spelling mistakes in all areas of her work as she now re-read her work and underlined words which did not 'look right'. She said the word aloud or to herself then used the class 'word bank' or a dictionary. Angela had recognised the generic use of an appropriate learning strategy.

Figure 7.1 The self-assessments of four pupils in a Y3 class

7.6 How can trainee teachers and NQTs move forward with MARRA?

Trainee teachers and NQTs can move forward with MARRA by building outwards, steadily and with increasing confidence, from the central relationship between teacher and pupil, through an understanding of home and school issues, to expectations at LEA and national levels.

Trainee teachers and NQTs should start by engaging with MARRA in practice by focusing upon the learning and learning needs of individual pupils. They should examine the similarities and differences between two pupils and ask questions. What were the learning objectives? What were the learning outcomes? How should these be recorded? Why do similarities and differences occur when pupils have experienced the same teaching? What prior knowledge, skills and understanding do the pupils bring to the learning situation? What should be the next steps in each pupil's learning? What should the next steps be in teaching the pupils?

Shared personal experiences of classroom practice enable trainee teachers and NQTs to gain a wider understanding of the reality of learning and how individual pupils' learning is affected by a range of social, physical and emotional factors. Case studies of classroom practice provide a focus for group discussion and encourage trainee teachers and NQTs to practise the key skills of observation, recording and reporting.

Beyond the classroom trainee teachers and NQTs should begin to engage in theoretical and practical aspects of MARRA. This may occur, for example, when critically analysing the validity of statutory tests and attempting to write questions which do not demonstrate bias, and when working with experienced teachers to moderate pupils' work in respect of the Attainment Target Level Descriptions. They should keep abreast of current developments and issues in assessment by reading the education press and academic journals and, if an Employment-Based Route trainee or an NQT, by attending INSET courses. Trainee teachers and NQTs can build their understanding by engaging with legislation and guidance from DfES, QCA, OFSTED, TTA and the LEA.

Trainee teachers and NQTs can combine theory and practice by talking to practitioners of their experiences and how each aspect of MARRA is undertaken in the school, from the role of the assessment coordinator to the teachers' attitudes and approaches to home–school communication.

Moving forward in MARRA requires teachers to have effective skills in each area, to know what is expected of them at different stages and by whom and, most importantly, to understand the purpose of monitoring, assessment, recording, reporting and accountability.

7.7 A final thought . . .

The opening chapter of this book stated that the purpose of MARRA is to enable learning, teaching and accountability through the effective use of assessment. It identified the processes involved in the planning and assessment cycles and stated the four purposes of assessment identified by TGAT – formative, diagnostic, summative and evaluative. The summative and evaluative purposes of assessment, assessment *of* learning, have dominated education legislation and guidance. The formative and diagnostic purposes of assessment, assessment *for* learning, have now been acknowledged as vital to the development of pupil learning and an essential feature of effective classroom practice.

Teaching and accountability have bowed to legislation, but no government can legislate for learning. Within such a tightly legislated framework it is often almost impossible to believe that the quality and provision of learning can be improved without legislation and guidance. Yet it can be, through the relationship between teacher and pupil.

MARRA is, first and foremost, about helping individual pupils to learn.

Appendices

Appendix A

Subject Monitoring Sheet

Subject:

Learning Objective	LO1:	LO2:	LO3:	LO4:	LO5:
Date					
Pupil A					
Pupil B					
Pupil C					
Pupil D					
Pupil E					
Pupil F					
Pupil G					
Pupil H					
Pupil I					
Pupil J					
Pupil K					
Pupil L					
Pupil M					
Pupil N					
Pupil O					
Pupil P					
Pupil Q					
Pupil R					
Pupil S					
Pupil T					
Pupil U					
Pupil V					
Pupil W					
Pupil X					
Pupil Y					
Pupil Z					
Notes					

Appendix B

Mark Monitoring Sheet

Item/Test																
Date																
Pupil A																
Pupil B																
Pupil C																
Pupil D																
Pupil E																
Pupil F																
Pupil G																
Pupil H																
Pupil I																
Pupil J																
Pupil K																
Pupil L																
Pupil M																
Pupil N																
Pupil O																
Pupil P																
Pupil Q																
Pupil R																
Pupil S																
Pupil T																
Pupil U																
Pupil V																
Pupil W																
Pupil X																
Pupil Y																
Pupil Z																
Notes																

Appendix C

General Assessment Sheet

Learning Objective:

Date:

Name	Comment
Pupil A	
Pupil B	
Pupil C	
Pupil D	
Pupil E	
Pupil F	
Pupil G	
Pupil H	
Pupil I	
Pupil J	
Pupil K	
Pupil L	
Pupil M	
Pupil N	
Pupil O	
Pupil P	
Pupil Q	
Pupil R	
Pupil S	
Pupil T	
Pupil U	
Pupil V	
Pupil W	
Pupil X	
Pupil Y	
Pupil Z	
Notes	

Appendix D

Focused Assessment Sheet

Subject:

Activity:

Date:

Learning Objective	LO1:	LO2:	LO3:
Pupil A			
Pupil B			
Pupil C			

Appendix E

Individual Pupil Record

Pupil Name:

Notes:

En:		Ma:		Sci:		ICT:	
Hi:	Ge:	Mu:	Art:	DT:	PE:	RE:	Gen:

Date	Subject and context	Comment and analysis	Target

Appendix F

Action Sheet

Date	Action to be taken	With	Date action taken

Glossary

Aim	What pupils should learn by the end of a given period of time such as a month or a term.
Attainment Target	Standards of pupil performance defined within the National Curriculum.
Benchmarking	Process by which schools compare their results with those of other schools of a similar nature.
Cold Marking	Marking which takes place away from the pupil.
Comparative Data	Data which compares pupil, school and national statutory assessment results.
Criterion-Referencing	Assessment measured against given criteria.
Diagnostic Assessment	Assessment which diagnoses learning difficulties.
End of Key Stage tests	Statutory tests which take place at the end of a Key Stage.
Evaluative Assessment	Assessment which enables evaluation of an organisation.
Evidence of Attainment	What to look for to determine whether learning has taken place.
Formative Assessment	Assessment which informs future teaching and learning.
Foundation Stage Profile	Statutory assessment that takes place before completion of the Foundation Stage.
Hot Marking	Marking which takes place with the pupil.
Ipsative-Referencing	Assessment measured against previous personal performance.
Learning Objective	What pupils should learn within a lesson.
Learning Outcome	What pupils actually learn.
Level Description	Assessment criteria used in Attainment Targets from 1995.
Metacognition	Learning how to learn.

Moderation	Process of agreeing judgement about pupils' work, often in relation to National Curriculum criteria.
National Curriculum Tests	Statutory tests which take place at the End of a Key Stage.
Norm-Referencing	Assessment measured against other pupils' results.
Performance Table	Published table of End of Key Stage results of schools within an LEA.
Record of Achievement	Cumulative portfolio of pupil's work celebrating achievement in and beyond the curriculum.
Standard Assessment Tasks	Term used for End of Key Stage assessments in 1991.
Standardised Test	Term used for End of Key Stage assessments in 1992.
Standard	A level of performance.
Statement of Attainment	Assessment criteria used in 1989 and 1991 National Curriculum Attainment Targets.
Statutory Assessment	Assessment which must be undertaken by law (e.g. End of Key Stage Assessment or assessment preceding a Statement of Special Educational Needs).
Summative Assessment	Assessment which summates learning.
Target	A next step in teaching or learning which is specific, challenging and attainable.
Teacher Assessment	End of Key Stage judgements made by the teacher, assigning Attainment Target levels to pupils' work.
Value Added	Measurement of the progress made by a pupil or a school.

References

Alexander, R., Rose, J. and Woodhead, C. (1992) *Curriculum Organisation and Classroom Practice in Primary Schools.* London: DfEE.

Ashman, A. and Conway, R. (1997) *An Introduction to Cognitive Education.* London: Routledge.

Askew, M. and Wiliam, D. (1995) *Recent Research in Mathematics Education 5–16.* London: Ofsted.

Ausubel, D. (1968) *Educational Psychology: A Cognitive View.* New York: Holt, Rinehart and Winston.

Bastiani, J. (1989) *Working with Parents: A Whole-School Approach.* Windsor: NFER-Nelson.

Bastiani, J. (1996) *Home–School Contracts and Agreements – Opportunity or Threat?* London: RSA.

BBC (2003) *World at One*, Radio 4, 28 February 2003.

Bennett, N. (1994) 'Managing learning in the primary school', in Bourne, J. (ed.) *Thinking Through Primary Practice.* Buckingham: Open University Press.

Berger, A., Buck, D. and Davis, V. (2001) *Assessing Pupils Performance Using the P-Levels*, London: David Fulton Publishers.

Black, P. (1998) *Testing: Friend or Foe?* London: Falmer Press.

Black, P. and Wiliam, D. (1998) *Inside the Black Box.* London: King's College.

Bliss, T. (1994) *Managing Children...Managing Themselves.* Bristol: Lucky Duck Publishing.

Bridges, D. (1994) 'Parents: customers or partners?', in Bridges, D. and McLauglin, T. (eds) *Education and the Market Place.* London: Falmer Press.

Brown, G. and Wragg, E. C. (1993) *Questioning.* London: Routledge.

Bryan, H. and Headington, R. (1998) 'Reconceptualising the roles of teachers and support staff', paper presented at European Conference on Educational Research, Ljubljana, Slovenia.

Buckinghamshire LEA (1993) *Teaching and Assessing Ma1 at Key Stage 1.* Aylesbury: Buckinghamshire LEA.

Cassell (1998) *Compact Dictionary.* London: Cassell.

Clarke, S. (1998) *Targeting Assessment in the Primary School.* London: Hodder and Stoughton.

Clarke, S. (2001) *Unlocking Formative Assessment.* London: Hodder and Stoughton.

Clay, M. (1993) *An Observation Survey of Early Literacy Achievement.* Portsmouth, NH: Heinemann.

Conner, C. (ed.) (1999) *Assessment in Action in the Primary School.* London: Falmer Press.

Daugherty, R. (1995) *National Curriculum Assessment: A Review of Policy 1987–1994.* London: Falmer Press.

Dean, G. (2001) *Challenging the More Able Language User,* 2nd edn. London: David Fulton Publishers.

Dearing, R. (1994) *The National Curriculum and its Assessment: Final Report.* London: SCAA.

DES (1988) *National Curriculum Task Group on Assessment and Testing: A Report.* London: DES.

DES (1991a) *Your Child and the National Curriculum.* London: DES.

DES (1991b) *The Parent's Charter: You and Your Child's Education.* London: DES.

DfE (1994a) *Final Report on the National Curriculum and its Assessment: The Government's Response.* London: HMSO.

DfE (1994b) *Our Children's Education: The Updated Parent's Charter.* London: DfE.

DfEE (1995) *The School Curriculum: A Brief Guide.* London: DfEE.

DfEE (1997a) *Excellence for All.* London: DfEE.

DfEE (1997b) *From Targets to Action.* London: DfEE.

DfEE (1998a) *Teaching: High Standards, High Status (Circular 4/98).* London: DfEE.

DfEE (1998b) *The National Literacy Strategy: A Framework For Teaching.* London: DfEE.

DfEE (1998c) *Target Setting in School (Circular 11/98).* London: DfEE.

DfEE (1999a) *The National Numeracy Strategy: A Framework For Teaching.* London: DfEE.

DfEE (1999b) *How is Your Child Doing at School?* London: DfEE.

DfEE (1999c) *It All Adds Up.* London: DfEE.

DfEE (1999d) *Autumn Package.* London: DfEE.

DfEE/QCA (1999) *The National Curriculum, Key Stages 1 and 2.* London: HMSO.

DfES (2001) *SEN Code of Practice.* London: DfES.

DfES (2003) *Raising Standards and Tackling Workload: A National Agreement.* London: DfES.

DfES/TTA (2002) *Qualifying to Teach: Professional Standards for Qualified Teacher Status.* London: TTA.

DfES/TTA (2003) *Induction Standards for Newly Qualified Teachers.* London: TTA.

Drummond, M. (1993) *Assessing Children's Learning.* London: David Fulton Publishers.

Eisner, E. W. (1985) *The Art of Educational Evaluation.* Lewes: Falmer Press.

Fisher, R. (1990) *Teaching Children to Think.* Cheltenham: Stanley Thornes.

Fountas, I. and Pinnell, G. (1996) *Guided Reading.* Portsmouth, NH: Heinemann.

Frost, R. (1999) 'Out of the mire: taming the beast that has become assessment', in Conner, C. (ed.) *Assessment in Action in the Primary School.* London: Falmer Press.

Galton, M. *et al.* (1999) *Inside the Primary Classroom: 20 Years On.* London: Routledge.

Gardner, P. (2002) *Strategies and Resources for Teaching and Learning in Inclusive Classrooms.* London: David Fulton Publishers.

Gipps, C. (1990) *Assessment: A Teacher's Guide to the Issues,* London: Hodder and Stoughton.

Gipps, C. (1994) *Beyond Testing.* London: Falmer Press.

Gipps, C. (1996) 'Assessment for learning', in Little, A. and Wolf, A. (eds) *Assessment in Transition: Learning, Monitoring and Selection an International Perspective.* Oxford: Pergamon Press.

Gipps, C. and Goldstein, H. (1983) *Monitoring Children: An Evaluation of the Assessment and Performance Unit.* London: Heinemann.

Glaser, R. (1995) 'Expert knowledge and the processes of thinking', in Murphy, P. *et al.* (eds) *Subject Learning in the Primary Currriculum.* London: Routledge.

Griffiths, A. and Hamilton, D. (1984) *Parent, Teacher, Child.* London: Methuen.

Hall, D. (2001) *Assessing the Needs of Bilingual Pupils: Living in Two Languages,* 2nd edn. London: David Fulton Publishers.

Harlen, W. (ed.) (1994) *Enhancing Quality in Assessment.* London: Paul Chapman Publishing.

Harlen, W. *et al.* (1992) 'Assessment and the improvement of education', *The Curriculum Journal* 3(3), 215–30.

Headington, R. and Howson, J. (1995) 'The school brochure: a marketing tool?', *Educational Management and Administration* 23(2), 89–95.

Hohmann, M., Banet, B. and Weikart, D. (1979) *Young Children in Action.* Ypsilanti, MI: High Scope Educational Research Foundation.

Hughes, M., Wikeley, F. and Nash, T. (1994) *Parents and Their Children's Schools.* Oxford: Blackwell.

James, C. and Phillips, P. (1995) 'The practice of educational marketing in schools', *Educational Management and Administration* 23(2), 75–88.

Jowett, S. and Baginsky, M. (1991) *Building Bridges: Parental Involvement in Schools.* London: Routledge.

Kingdon, M. (1995) 'External marking: the KS2/KS3 tests in 1995', *British Journal of Curriculum and Assessment* **5**(2), 12–17.

Koshy, V. (2000) *Teaching Mathematics to Able Children*. London: David Fulton Publishers.

Kounin, J. S. (1970) *Discipline and Group Management in Classrooms*. New York: Holt, Rinehart and Winston.

Kyriacou, C. (1995) *Essential Teaching Skills*. Cheltenham: Stanley Thornes.

Lawton, D. and Gordon, P. (1987) *HMI*. London: Routledge.

Lindsay, G. (1998) 'Baseline assessment: a positive or malign initiative?', in Norwich, B. and Lindsey, G. (eds) *Baseline Assessment: Benefits and Pitfalls*. Tamworth: NASEN.

Lindsay, G. and Desforges, M. (1998) *Baseline Assessment: Practice, Problems and Possibilities*. London: David Fulton Publishers.

Maclure, J. S. (1968) *Educational Documents: England and Wales 1816–1967*. London: Methuen.

Maclure, S. (1992) *Education Re-formed*. London: Hodder and Stoughton.

McCallum, B. (1996) 'The transfer and use of assessment information between primary and secondary schools', *British Journal of Curriculum and Assessment* **6**(3), 10–14.

McCallum, B. *et al.* (1995) 'National Curriculum assessment: emerging models of teacher assessment in the classroom', in Torrance, H. (ed.) *Evaluating Authentic Assessment*. Buckingham: Open University Press.

McGarvey, B. *et al.* (1996) 'A Study of auxiliary support in some primary classrooms: extra hands and extra eyes', *Educational Research* **38**(3), 293–305.

McNess, E. *et al.* (2001) 'The changing nature of assessment in English primary classrooms: findings from the PACE Project 1989–1997', *Education 3–13* **29**, 3, 9–16.

Merttens, R. and Vass, J. (1990) *Sharing Maths Cultures*. Basingstoke: Falmer Press.

Mortimore, P. (1996) 'Quality control in education and schools', in Craft, A. (ed.) *Primary Education: Assessing and Planning Learning*. London: Routledge.

Moyles, J. and Suschitzky, W. (1997) *Classroom Assistants in KS1 Classes*. London: Association of Teachers and Lecturers.

Newby, M. (1996) 'Learning objectives in perspective', *British Journal of Curriculum and Assessment* **6**(3), 43–5.

Nisbet, J. and Shucksmith, J. (1986) *Learning Strategies*. London: Routledge.

Nurse, A. D. and Headington, R. (1999) 'Balancing the needs of children, parents and teachers', in David, T. (ed.) *Young Children Learning*. London: Paul Chapman Publishing.

OFSTED (1996a) *Subjects and Standards. Issues for School Development Arising from OFSTED Inspection Findings 1994–5*. London: HMSO.

OFSTED (1996b) *The Teaching of Reading in 45 Inner London Primary Schools.* London: HMSO.

OFSTED (1998) *Teacher Assessment in the Core Subjects at Key Stage Two.* London: HMSO.

Plowden, B. (1967) *Children and Their Primary Schools.* London: HMSO.

Pollard, A. (2002) *Reflective Teaching: Effective and Evidence-Informed Professional Practice.* London: Continuum.

Pollitt, A. (2000) *The Key Stage 3 Dip.* London: QCA.

Pring, R. (1996) 'Standards and quality in education', in Craft, A. (ed.) *Primary Education: Assessing and Planning Learning.* London: Routledge.

Pye, J. (1988) *Invisible Children.* Oxford: Oxford University Press.

QCA (1998a) *Key Stage 1 Assessment and Reporting Arrangements 1999.* London: QCA.

QCA (1998b) *Key Stage 2 Assessment and Reporting Arrangements 1999.* London: QCA.

QCA (1999a) *Early Learning Goals.* London: QCA.

QCA (1999b) *Key Stage 1 Assessment and Reporting Arrangements 2000.* London: QCA.

QCA (1999c) *Key Stage 2 Assessment and Reporting Arrangements 2000.* London: QCA.

QCA (1999d) *Standards at Key Stage 1: English and Mathematics.* London: QCA.

QCA (1999e) *Standards at Key Stage 2: English, Mathematics and Science.* London: QCA.

QCA (2000) *A Language in Common: Assessing English as an Additional Language.* London: QCA.

QCA (2002) *Key Stage 1 Assessment and Reporting Arrangements 2003,* London: QCA.

Reynolds, D. and Farrell, S. (1996) *Worlds Apart? A Review of International Surveys of Educational Achievement Involving England.* London: Ofsted.

Richards, C. (2001) 'Cutting PANDAs down to size?' *Education 3–13* **29**, 3, 22–38.

Sadler, R. (1989) 'Formative assessment and the design of instructional systems', *Instructional Science* **18**, 119–44.

SCAA (1993) *School Assessment Folder: Key Stage 1.* London: SCAA.

SCAA (1995) *English: Exemplification of Standards Key Stages 1 and 2.* London: SCAA.

SCAA (1996a) *Desirable Outcomes for Children's Learning on Entering Compulsory Education.* London: SCAA.

SCAA (1996b) *Promoting Continuity Between Key Stage 2 and Key Stage 3.* London: SCAA.

SCAA (1997a) *Key Stage 2 Mental Arithmetic Pilot Test.* London: SCAA.

SCAA (1997b) *Baseline Assessment Scales.* London: SCAA.

SCAA (1997c) *National Framework for Baseline Assessment.* London: SCAA.

SCAA (1997d) *Making Effective Use of the Key Stage 2 Assessments.* London: SCAA.

SCAA (1997e) *Target Setting and Benchmarking in Schools: Consultation Paper.* London: SCAA.

SEAC (1990a) *A Guide to Teacher Assessment: Pack C.* London: SEAC.

SEAC (1990b) *Records of Achievement in Primary Schools.* London: SEAC.

SEAC (1991) *Assessment Record Booklet.* London: SEAC.

SEAC (1993) *Children's Work Assessed.* London: SEAC.

Shorrocks-Taylor, D. (1999) *National Testing: Past, Present and Future.* Leicester: British Psychological Society.

Skemp, R. (1989) *Mathematics in the Primary School.* London: Routledge.

Stow, W. (1997) 'Concept mapping: a tool for self-assessment?', *Primary Science Review* **49**, 12–16.

Sutton, R. (1991) *Assessment: A Framework for Teachers.* London: Routledge.

Swaffield, S. (1999) 'The Role of the LEA in Supporting Assessment in the Primary School', in Conner, C. (ed.) *Assessment in Action in the Primary School.* London: Falmer Press.

TES (1995a) 'Survey vindicates key stage test markers', *Times Educational Supplement,* 11 August.

TES (1995b) 'One in seven sends back test papers', *Times Educational Supplement,* 1 September.

TES (1998) 'Tests are unreliable says chief inspector', *Times Educational Supplement,* 18 December.

TES (1999a) 'Did spider tests raise boys' scores?', *Times Educational Supplement,* 15 October.

TES (1999b) 'Many parents "afraid" to speak to teachers', *Times Educational Supplement,* 10 December.

TES (2000a) 'Keep it short and simple for boys', *Times Educational Supplement,* 14 January.

TES (2000b) 'Class bias of national tests', *Times Educational Supplement,* 28 January.

Thomas, G. (1992) *Effective Classroom Teamwork: Support or Intrusion?* London: Routledge.

Torrance, H. and Pryor, J. (1998) *Investigating Formative Assessment.* Buckingham: Open University Press.

TTA (2000) *Career Entry Profile.* London: TTA.

Tymms, P. (1998) 'Discussant's paper', in Norwich, B. and Lindsey, G. (eds) *Baseline Assessment: Benefits and Pitfalls.* Tamworth: NASEN.

Tymms, P. (1999) *Baseline Assessment and Monitoring in Primary Schools.* London: David Fulton Publishers.

Tymms, P. and Henderson, B. (1996) *The Value Added National Project: Technical Report*. London: SCAA.

Vygotsky, L. S. (1978) *Mind in Society*. Cambridge, MA: Harvard University Press.

Walker, R. and Adelman, C. (1976) 'Strawberries', in Stubbs, M. and Delamont, S. (eds) *Explorations in Classroom Observation*. Chichester: Wiley.

Wedell, K. (1998) 'Discussant's paper', in Norwich, B. and Lindsey, G. (eds) *Baseline Assessment: Benefits and Pitfalls*. Tamworth: NASEN.

White, R. and Gunstone, R. (1992) *Probing Understanding*. New York: Falmer Press.

Wiliam, D. and Black, P. (2002) 'Feedback is the best nourishment', in *Mind Measuring, Times Educational Supplement*, 4 October 2002.

Williams, E. (2002) 'Over to you', in *Mind Measuring, Times Educational Supplement*, 4 October 2002.

Wood, D. (1988) *How Children Think and Learn*. Oxford: Blackwell.

Wragg, E. C. (ed.) (1984) *Classroom Teaching Skills*. London: Routledge.

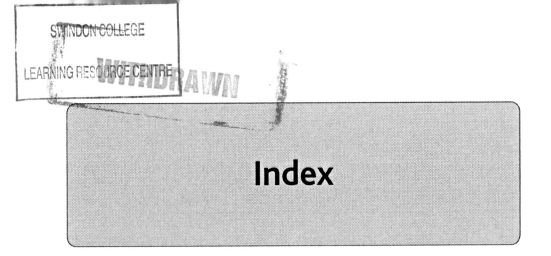

Index

Subject Index

Author Index

Printed in the United Kingdom
by Lightning Source UK Ltd.
109029UKS00003B/209-360

9 781853 469626